"*Braving the Future* offers penetrating insights into what Scripture has to say about work, creation, and personhood as well as faithful analysis of our tech-saturated world. We can rely on Estes to guide us toward Christian fidelity in the face of unprecedented technological changes."

—TODD A. WILSON, PRESIDENT OF THE CENTER FOR PASTOR THEOLOGIANS

"*Braving the Future* is a seriously important book. As new technologies invade every space and hour of our shared lives, Douglas Estes argues that Christians must reject the temptations to embrace them uncritically or reject them outright."

—BRUCE RILEY ASHFORD, PROVOST AND PROFESSOR AT SOUTHEASTERN BAPTIST THEOLOGICAL SEMINARY

"Douglas Estes is a master writer. His work provides valuable cultural analysis on our use of tech, both now and into the future. His unique voice at this nexus is not one to ignore."

—REBECCA RANDALL, SCIENCE EDITOR AT *CHRISTIANITY TODAY*

"Douglas Estes offers us, in the face of fear, an angelic word: 'Do not be afraid.' Even better, he offers us a theocentric word in this wonderful and timely book: that God will be with us in the future that our technologies create, however marvelous or terrifying those technologies may be."

—W. DAVID O. TAYLOR, ASSISTANT PROFESSOR OF THEOLOGY AND CULTURE AT FULLER THEOLOGICAL SEMINARY

"In *Braving the Future*, Douglas Estes develops a scaffold for theological reflection on our current but constantly changing technological landscape. Most profoundly, Estes reminds us that however our technological future emerges, God is present, God loves us, and God remains committed to our redemption."

—QUENTIN KINNISON, PROGRAM DIRECTOR OF CHRISTIAN MINISTRY AND LEADERSHIP AT FRESNO PACIFIC UNIVERSITY

"Instead of hiding out or blindly accepting every new technology, we must educate ourselves. Thankfully, Douglas Estes has written this excellent resource to help us understand our quickly advancing world of technology. Filled with solid research, Scripture, and thought-provoking ideas, *Braving the Future* shows us how to evaluate new tech with a Christian perspective."

—ARLENE PELLICANE, AUTHOR OF *CALM, COOL, AND CONNECTED*

"Douglas Estes demonstrates how even the most astounding innovations will continue to point humanity toward God and reveal God's love for us. *Braving the Future* is an essential guidebook for any person of faith and will become ever more important in the coming years."

—DORCAS CHENG-TOZUN, AUTHOR OF *START, LOVE, REPEAT*

"*Braving the Future* guides us to see how technology is simultaneously making the world better and offering new versions of old idols. Douglas Estes combines nuance with both scriptural fidelity and clear writing, making this the first-stop guide for faithfully navigating the rapidly changing technological world."

—JOSHUA CHATRAW, RESIDENT THEOLOGIAN AT HOLY TRINITY ANGLICAN CHURCH AND AUTHOR OF *APOLOGETICS AT THE CROSS*

"Douglas Estes's *Braving the Future* is a must-read. We desperately need to better understand the profound significance of technology today from a theological point of view. Is there an undeniable, profound, and radical connection between technology and spirituality? The answer to this question is crucial for our future."

—ANTONIO SPADARO, SJ, EDITOR OF *LA CIVILTÀ CATTOLICA* AND AUTHOR OF *CYBERTHEOLOGY*

"*Braving the Future* calls for new conversations about the theological implications of a future filled with artificial intelligence, drones, robots, virtual reality, and more. Estes deftly weaves together biblical insight and Christian theology with a critical perspective on technology, and he uses these future visions to ask big questions about what it means to be human today."

—TIM HUTCHINGS, AUTHOR OF *CREATING CHURCH ONLINE*

"Tackling the issues surrounding transhumanism in our age of technology is no small task. Douglas Estes offers the Christian community a guide and leads us to think about questions raised from transhumanism in a fresh way, showing us our need for the perfect being—namely, the God of Christian theism."

—JOSHUA R. FARRIS, ASSISTANT PROFESSOR OF THEOLOGY AT HOUSTON BAPTIST UNIVERSITY

"Douglas Estes's *Braving the Future* is so greatly needed because it provides a theological entryway into the technological world in which we live. The issues Estes addresses are no longer confined to the musings of science fiction, and the thoughtful, innovative work presented in this volume allows Christians to consider what it means to participate fully in the redemptive purposes of Jesus."

—CHRISTOPHER BENEK, PASTOR AND CEO OF THE COCREATORS NETWORK

"How should Christians live in a world of seemingly unceasing technological advances? I'm not always excited about the impact that these technologies have on the home and the church. This is why I'm grateful for *Braving the Future*. This book is a helpful and clear conversation partner as we brave the future with confidence in God."

—CHRIS BRUNO, ASSISTANT PROFESSOR OF NEW TESTAMENT AND GREEK AT BETHLEHEM COLLEGE AND SEMINARY

Herald Press
PO Box 866, Harrisonburg, Virginia 22803
www.HeraldPress.com

Library of Congress Cataloging-in-Publication Data
Names: Estes, Douglas, author.
Title: Braving the future : Christian faith in a world of limitless tech /
Douglas Estes.
Description: Harrisonburg : Herald Press, 2018. | Includes bibliographical
references.
Identifiers: LCCN 2018035062| ISBN 9781513803258 (pbk. : alk. paper) | ISBN
9781513803265 (hardcover : alk. paper)
Subjects: LCSH: Technology--Religious aspects--Christianity.
Classification: LCC BR115.T42 E88 2018 | DDC 261.5/6--dc23 LC record avail-
able at https://lccn.loc.gov/2018035062

BRAVING THE FUTURE
© 2018 by Herald Press, Harrisonburg, Virginia 22803. 800-245-7894.
     All rights reserved.
Library of Congress Control Number: 2018035062
International Standard Book Number: 978-1-5138-0325-8 (paperback);
     978-1-5138-0326-5 (hardcover); 978-1-5138-0327-2 (ebook)
Printed in United States of America
Cover and interior design by Reuben Graham

22 21 20 19 18   10 9 8 7 6 5 4 3 2 1

BRAVING THE FUTURE

CHRISTIAN FAITH IN A WORLD OF LIMITLESS TECH

DOUGLAS ESTES

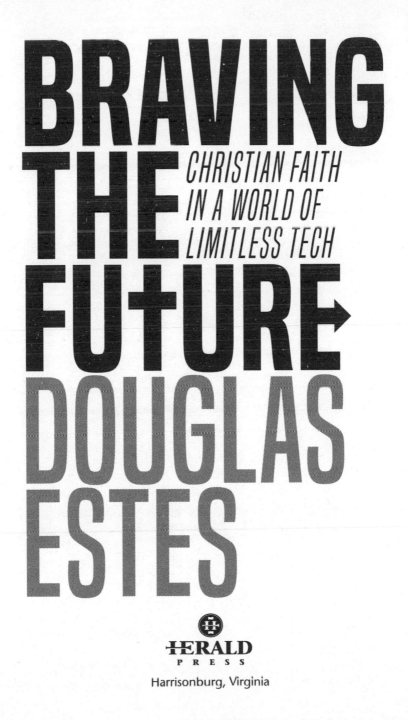

HERALD PRESS

Harrisonburg, Virginia

for Everett

CONTENTS

GOD, PEOPLE, TECH

What is the future? In the simplest sense, it is the time that lies ahead. For many of us, the future is something to which we look forward. Thinking about the future may conjure up images of wondrous technological advances on the near horizon: flying cars, talking robots, and wonders in a pill. These incredible technologies promise to make life easier, more enjoyable, and last longer. Eighty will be the new forty, one hundred the new eighty, and the world will be at our fingertips (virtually, at least).

Just think about all the awesome improvements to life in the past twenty years alone: Robotic vacuums. LED light bulbs. Ebook readers. Functional MRI. Flat panel TVs. DNA ancestry testing. Bluetooth speakers. Portable defibrillators. GPS. Digital SLR cameras. Blu-ray discs. Internet news. Lithium-ion rechargeable batteries. Digital video recorders. Satellite radio. Social media. 3D printers. Smartphones. Drones. Retinal implants. Fidget spinners.

All these and more in just twenty short years! Imagine what the next twenty years will bring. "The future's so bright" goes the old song. And it's true enough.

Wait, some will insist. What about killer robots, antibiotic-resistant bacteria, and climate change? Won't these things potentially ruin our future? And what about increases in personal immorality, corporate greed, nations at war, and the overall turning away from God that we see in the world at large? Surely these are signs that the future may not be so rosy after all.[1]

Yet the world keeps on humming along, and our view of the future doesn't seem to be too dimmed by it all. We may worry a little about artificial intelligence, but we are so looking forward to trying the newest virtual reality headset. We may have some apprehensions about antibiotic-resistant bacteria, but once we can have our groceries delivered by drone to our doorsteps, our lives will be so much easier. We may be generally concerned about the planet, but once we finally make free Wi-Fi a basic human right, our planet will truly be a better place. Go ahead and re-queue that "future's so bright" song.

Where does this optimism about the future come from? Why, when we think of the future, do we have visions of tech-marvels dancing in our heads? Here in the West, we tend to look forward to the future; it is not something that we fear.

But we do not base our general optimism about the future purely on facts. As we will discuss in this book, some evidence does point to a bright future for our world. Yet much of our optimism about the future comes from culture more than from science, faith, or anything else.

For the past several hundred years, modern philosophy and popular culture have worked together to condition us Westerners to believe the world is moving in the right direction. Yes, horrific wars, terrible plagues, appalling injustices, and an incalculable number of smaller problems have occurred in the past few centuries. Yet none of these seemed to stymie cultural attitudes for long. American politicians and personalities can speak of being on the "right side of history" since history is moving steadily toward the good (or at least toward their own agendas).[2] As a whole, people believe the world is becoming a better place.

We may fear economic uncertainty, political turmoil, nuclear war, or ecological damage, but we do not fear the future itself. This is why—for better or worse—doomsayers predicting a nuclear conflagration or environmental catastrophe do not gain much traction in our culture. The future is ours; it is our destiny.

This general optimism that people in the West feel about the future is a somewhat recent development. For much of recorded history, culture promoted the opposite of what it promotes today—our hope was in our past. In the cultures and times that antedate ours, people viewed the past as reliable, filled with good examples for the way we are to live our lives. The great deeds of ages past were sacred events that would never be repeated but that we could hope to model. In this cultural perspective, the future did not carry anything for people to look forward to. To them, the past was golden, but the future was uncertain and worrying. In fact, even the idea of "the future," as we understand it today, is a modern spin on what lies ahead.

What changed? Food, for one. Most people born in our world today—certainly in the West—are born into a world in which food is readily accessible. This was not the case for those earlier cultures. In their world, one without supermarkets and grocery stores, food was always in limited supply. No one could be certain that they would have enough food next month or next week. Famine was always a possibility. Today I know if I go to the grocery store, it will always have food.

From our perspective, the past is out of date, the present is changing rapidly, and the future is bigger and bolder than we could ever imagine. The world seems to be spinning on its axis faster than ever before. The speed of technological change seems on the verge of being too fast for us to keep track. If Bob Dylan were a millennial, the changin' he'd sing about today might be technological as much as social. That's because the greatest changes the world faces today are those coming from technological advances.

And they are coming fast.

ESCAPING THE PAST

Think for a moment of the names and faces of your grandparents, or your great-grandparents if you know them. Most of us can see them in our mind's eye, smiling at us from the past. Each of them had different names and came from different places. Some were laborers, some were soldiers, some were seamstresses, some were slaves. But there is one thing that every one of them had in common: They were lucky to live past childhood.

We might be tempted to think that the end of the nineteenth century was pretty modern. It had steam locomotives, film cameras, telephones, and vaccines. Yet it also had a staggeringly high infant mortality rate. For example, about 20 percent of all babies born in Boston in the 1870s did not survive their first year.[3] For those who did survive the first year, at least as many as those who had died as babies did not survive childhood.[4] In short, if you had been born in Boston in the latter half of the nineteenth century, you had not much more than a 50 percent chance of making it into adulthood.[5] If you did, you were one of the lucky ones.

There is no way someone born and raised in the West today can grasp the magnitude of this. As one demographer writes, "How populations and societies could cope with appalling mortality levels, managing to survive, reproduce, expand, and accumulate, is still a matter of wonder."[6] During the latter half of the nineteenth century, every birth was high risk.

Only our ancestors born in the twentieth century had science, not luck, on their side. My paternal grandparents were born at the tail end of the nineteenth century, a time in which the percentage of infant deaths began to drop rapidly. The advantages they had in terms of improved sanitation, better understanding of hygiene, single-family home construction, and prenatal exams directly contributed to their likelihood of survival.[7] For example, one technological marvel my grandparents had ready access to that their grandparents did not was soap. That's right: soap. Though soap was invented before recorded history and the wealthy used it sporadically, it wasn't until the mid-nineteenth century that people started using it regularly to improve personal hygiene.[8] It strains our understanding of history to think of nineteenth-century people riding on trains, getting their photos taken, and using telephones—all while still questioning the technological advancement of soap. No one said technological progress was even. Just look at the century in which we now live, in which we can make the blind see but cannot heal teeth or stop the common cold.

Can I say what we are all thinking? I, for one, am glad that I was born in the twentieth century instead of the nineteenth. And I am glad that my children were born in the twenty-first century. Unlike my grandparents, and certainly my great-grandparents, I know that my children stand an excellent chance of living long—and I pray, meaningful—lives. I cannot wrap my mind around the deplorable conditions that existed just a few centuries ago—and that remain in some places around the world—in which technology was and is limited. I can admit that I am very thankful for technology. In many ways, we can pause and be thankful for all the ways that tech has improved our lives and made the world a better place.

BRAVING THE FUTURE

Compared to the past, the world in which we now live is a world of marvels, and it's getting more marvelous by the day. The future is coming so fast now that we can only imagine what it will bring. This acceleration, though, creates a problem. What happens when technology advances at such a speed that the average person can no longer keep up? Some futurists believe that later in this century, or maybe early in the next, technological advancement will increase so quickly that no one will be able to keep track of it.[9] A few believe this pace will occur in the next thirty years.

In this scenario, technological advancement will largely move from humans into the hands of quantum computing and artificial intelligence. When this happens, our way of life will change more dramatically than humanity has ever experienced before. Think of it as trying to explain an iMac to a medieval peasant. Maybe worse.

Let me make it personal. My father spent his whole career as an engineer at NASA. His area was earth-to-space communications. He worked on the Gemini, Mercury, and Apollo missions. He was peripherally involved in the greatest technological feat that humanity has ever accomplished. He understood technology in a way that probably 99 percent of the population in his day did not.

After he retired, I bought him a personal computer with Windows and a mouse. He couldn't grasp it. He never did come to understand how to use a personal computer before he passed away. He could, however, tell me stories about computer rooms with vacuum tubes. I shudder to think how technologically ignorant I will be compared to my grandchildren.

This radical technological jump—a leap of such scale that the average person won't be able to keep up—may or may not be imminent and cause for concern. What we do need to concern ourselves with now is how technology today is rapidly changing the way we live and the way we relate to each other. The questions at the heart of this book are: How do we handle rapid technological change? How do we evaluate new tech in light of what the Bible teaches and what Jesus models for us? How do we discern the best use of tech that has not yet even arrived? How do we remain faithful to God during a technological turning point in history?

As people who follow God and wish to live well in this world, Christians sometimes get painted as being against science and against technology.[10] I have not found this to be the case. I love science, and I am very excited about technology. Most of the Christians I meet feel largely the same way. But this stereotype exists for two reasons.

First, many people of faith are not against science or technology per se; they simply do not accept everything science says and technology does just because science says it and technology does it. As much as I love science, scientists have come to occupy the role of priests in our society. Scientists make pronouncements of truth as if from on high, and people are expected to follow their lead. Among the general population, most people do just that. In contrast, Christians do not see scientists as their priests (as we have a superior High Priest), and we are sometimes slower to accept new pronouncements. We ask questions about tech that other groups don't always think to ask—questions that may seem impertinent to the priests of science and technology. If I let my five-year-old use a smartphone, how will it affect her behavior? How much time should we let our kids spend online? Which kinds of websites does the school library block and not block? What are we no longer doing now that we spend so much time on social media? Christians aren't the only ones who ask questions like these, but we do tend to raise them more frequently.

Second, many people of faith question some of the underlying ideas that are often promoted along with scientific achievement and technological advancement. When these ideas and their objections collide, popular culture can make it appear that Christians object to the science or the technology itself.

But technology, in and of itself, does not present an existential threat to Christian faith. Neither does the use of technology, in and of itself, present such a threat. This does not mean that all technology and its uses are uniformly healthy; it just means that Christians in general do not and should not object to the use of technology in general.

Could this change? Many people are aware that the Amish are a community who eschew most modern technology. As technology increases, should other Christians object to rapid technological change by following the path of the Amish? Wouldn't we all be happier and more faithful if we aspired to lives that focus on community and God instead of the latest contraption? Some may wonder if Christians should take such a stand now, before it is too late.

But it *is* too late. Even if a subsection of society—whether Christian, anarchist, or other—wanted to stop the growth of technology, it wouldn't work. At this point the rapid growth of technology is inevitable.[11] It's going to happen whether one group wants it to or not. One reason is that the marvels of technology have captured the imagination of the world. Once people imagine it, they want it, and there is no easy way to prevent it. Once the genie is out of the bottle, it won't go back in (at least not without a fight).

When CFL light bulbs first came on the market I was intrigued, but after using one I didn't care for them. From the color of light they produced to the trace amounts of mercury within the easily broken bulb, CFLs just did not live up to the hype. In contrast, when LED bulbs hit the market, I really had to have them. Why? Because in my imagination, I was able to see myself outfitting my house with bulbs that faithfully mimicked an incandescent bulb, saved energy, and lasted a third of a lifetime.

Last year, after no small amount of coveting on my part, I finally bought an LED bulb that can change colors via Bluetooth control from my smartphone. When my kids need to get their wiggles out, we put the bulb in our living room light fixture and signal it to go crazy as the music starts to play. Instant dance party and, in an hour, tuckered-out kids. Isn't technology grand?

There's another reason that technology is inevitable: money. The force that drives our modern world more than anything else is economic growth.[12] Before the modern era, economic growth was built on people—agriculture and industrialization.

As the population grows in the twenty-first century, industrialization will continue to decline and agriculture will continue to produce greater amounts of food in less space with fewer resources. As a result, the engines of the world's economy will increasingly center on technology and information. In 2020, Apple will create the next iWhatever™—not because they are passionate about technology (though they are), but because they want to make money. Also, if they don't produce new technology, lots of people won't have jobs and economies will collapse. Instead of gold and ivory, gadgetry and data are becoming the primary commodities of the twenty-first century.

THE WORLD TODAY

"So flying cars are coming soon?" the skeptic asks. Maybe. Maybe not. That is the challenge of the future—we really don't know what the future holds when it comes to the details. Benjamin Franklin, a proponent of technology, famously regretted that cryogenic freezing would perhaps not be available before he died of old age.[13] Yes, you read that right: Franklin, who played with electricity but didn't understand soap technology, thought it possible that dead people might be frozen for future resuscitation in his lifetime. Unfortunately for Franklin, he was off by several centuries; there is no indication we are close to that technology even in the early part of the twenty-first century.

The flying car keeps all futurists honest. No one knows exactly where technology is heading. On the flip side, there is the internet. No one saw that coming. Just think back to the original *Star Trek* episodes—Jim Kirk had a circa-2008 flip phone to call his ship—but he had no way to Google for information. Spock was the Google. Back in 1966, popular science fiction could envision a handheld communication device, but it couldn't envision an information network. Though the rate of technological progress seems more and more exponential, it is certainly not smooth. Technology leaps forward in one area but slows in another. Flying cars and cryogenic freezing will have to wait. In the next century, new and unpredicted technologies will appear and will create major societal shifts in the same way soap, the automobile, and the internet did.

We may not be able to peer into the details about the future, but we don't need to. No matter what technological advances come our way in the next few decades, we can be ready now in our understanding of how God can lead us in the midst of a rapidly changing world.

One of the difficulties with discussing technology lies in the divide between the practical and the philosophical. There is the practical part of it: How much time should we let our kids be on screens or social media? Should we edit out a possibly destructive gene from our unborn child? Then there is the philosophical part: What posture should we take toward new technology? What are the theological ramifications of technology for the world or the church? The purpose of *Braving the Future* is to help us think through some of the philosophical parts so that we are better informed and ready to apply them more meaningfully to the practical part of our lives. If we focus only on the practical, then many of the arguments quickly change and we won't cover much. Plus, practical questions that arise naturally with each new technology make it easy to get lost in the trees and not take time to wonder about the forest.

This is not to say that discernment around the practical aspect of technology is not important. Many wonderful books offer readers practical suggestions on managing technology;

these include Andy Crouch's *The Tech-Wise Family* and Brian Housman's *Tech Savvy Parenting*.[14] But *Braving the Future* is different. Instead of helping families and individuals navigate immediate questions about technology use, this book opens a discussion about the philosophical and theological issues that future tech will bring with it. That way, when this tech arrives, you will be prepared to face it in a proactive, not reactive, manner.

Before we step onto the platform, there are three areas in which we'll build a preliminary foundation for the discussion: God, people, and technology.

God.

Our starting point for discussion is the biblical and creedal view of God. This view is held by Christians around the world and forms a basic foundation that we can trace back over the centuries to the early church. For this we give thanks, because God is good, and his love endures forever (see Psalm 136:1).

Along with God's goodness, we want to affirm eight specific descriptions of God that will serve as the basis for much of our discussion. We'll explore one of these divine attributes in each of the chapters in the book:

1. God is totally capable; God doesn't need help from people.
2. God is master of his own destiny; God doesn't flounder about with uncertainty.
3. God is in control of all that goes on in our world; God doesn't ever relinquish that.
4. God knows everything there is to know; God doesn't get caught unaware.

5. God is present in every corner of the universe; God isn't restricted to one place or time.
6. God has full power over everything; God has no limit to what he can do.
7. God is totally perfect, not making mistakes; God doesn't sin or do wrong.
8. God is eternal; God doesn't have a beginning or an end.[15]

For some readers, these descriptions may seem pretty basic. That's good, because agreement on the basic nature of these theological descriptions about God will make navigating the technological explosion that much more manageable. Of course, these are not the only descriptions we can use to describe God; God's character is also loving and gracious and kind, for example. But the attributes listed here are among the ones most often used by theologians to describe God, and they will become surprisingly relevant as we consider future tech.

People.

Created in the image of God, we as humans rebelled and messed everything up. Then we kept on rebelling at every possible opportunity. We long for God, wish we were God, but never, ever live up to God's great expectations for our lives. We need God to rescue us, whether we are willing to admit it or not.

If we look at people horizontally, from others' perspectives, people are a real mixed bag. James makes a great case for this when he points out, in essence, that people can both sing the "Hallelujah Chorus" from Handel's Messiah and savage each other in a Twitter war (see James 3:9). If we can be so inconsistent with our mouths, just think how inconsistent we can be with our hands and feet. This inconsistency is our hitch. We are both awful sinners and yet made for so much more. In a weird way, both the sinners-in-the-hands-of-an-angry-God Puritan pastor Jonathan Edwards and the everything-is- awesome televangelist Joel Osteen are, generally speaking, correct. We are broken, and yet God wants to do great things through us. This is not due to anything we have done; it simply reflects the greatness of God's creation of us, and our utter downfall in rejecting our Creator. Any theology that doesn't account for both our depravity and our potential is lacking.

In order to account for all this, and to cope with living in our broken world, people have created all sorts of philosophies and ideologies. Some of these are good, some are bad; most can go either way depending on circumstances. One of the ideas that has become quite commonplace in our modern world is sometimes referred to as "the religion of humanity."[16] What this means is that instead of putting their trust in God (or even a god), many modern people see human beings as the greatest thing in the universe and think, therefore, that we should put our faith and trust in humanity. This view is known as *humanism*. Instead of turning to God to determine the course of their lives, many people turn to themselves (or other people) to discover what is true for themselves. Many modern people worship their own greatness instead of the greatness of God.[17] This "religion" started taking the West by storm (literally: look at the French Revolution) a little more than two hundred years ago. This cultural revolution happened in part as a rejection of the Christian faith. This self-love fest continues up until our present day.

By the twenty-first century, the idea that humanity is the end-all and be-all of our universe has started to wane. It has run its course, as all ill-conceived philosophies do. At the beginning of the twenty-first century, our culture is poised to embrace something new. One of the major philosophies vying for position suggests that humanity is on the verge of evolving into its next phase. As a result of hitting that exponential curve of technological advancement, people will start changing so quickly that they will be more *unlike* people from the premodern era than like them.

This view of life is known as *transhumanism*, or *H+*, and sometimes referred to as *technohumanism* or *posthumanism* (although posthumanism is more commonly reserved for a different philosophy also popular today). Maybe you have never heard of any of these terms, but our culture has already exposed you to the ideas behind them, and you have surely felt the effects. Transhumanism is one of the main ingredients baked into the cake of many Hollywood movies from *X-Men* to *Transcendence*. It is a philosophy designed to help make sense of all the rapid tech change.[18] Some thinkers anticipate it will be the biggest philosophical and cultural force in the twenty-first century.[19]

In this view, natives of the early twentieth century were People 1.0, but by the twenty-second century, everyone will get a full upgrade to People 2.0 hardware (and maybe software). An early proponent, Julian Huxley, writes, "The human species can, if it wishes, transcend itself—not just sporadically, an individual here in one way, an individual there in another way, but in its entirety, as humanity."[20] This view takes humanity's self-love from merely an emotional expression to physical demonstration: Humanity will evolve itself into a whole new species.

Think of it like this. Let's assume technology continues its upward climb along an exponential curve into the next century.

Citizens of the twenty-second century may expect to live 150 years, communicate without effort with everything and everyone, have instant recall of all memories, and spend their time pursuing knowledge and leisure (albeit without flying cars). What does a 130-year-old from 2178—who spends his days designing intricate garden structures for robotic application and his nights watching reruns of his hijinks as a twenty-year-old in the 2070s—have in common with a thirty-year-old from 1834—who plowed the field by hand, didn't understand soap, and likely had only a few years left to live?

To what point we embrace these new humanistic philosophies is not important at this stage. What *is* important is to understand how they affect people. Ideas that are fit for the times are promoted through culture. Postmodern philosophy and popular culture will ensure many people believe these new philosophies—an abundance of evidence exists in Hollywood movies, videogames, and the news media.[21] During the modern era, Western culture so loudly trumpets the idea that humanity is the greatest that it is hard not to buy into it. (Just note the shift from Edwards to Osteen; from "fly from the wrath to come" to *Your Best Life Now*, respectively.)[22] In the same way, culture is poised to broadcast the idea that it's time for humanity to evolve to the next level. That evolution will change us in remarkable ways.

Technology.

A final point here is about technology itself. Generally speaking, technology is good in that it improves our lives and makes the world a better place. When I pronounce technology "good," I don't mean "good" in the same way God meant "good" in the book of Genesis. Instead, I mean "good" in the sense of useful and worthwhile. Technology is good in the way that ice cream and hugs are good. I also don't mean every application of technology is "good" in this sense; sonic cannons and selfie sticks can be good in some applications and bad in others.

Let's dig a little deeper into this. Two basic views describe how technology relates to people. The first view is that technology is simply a tool that people can use. In its nature, a piece of technology is neither good or bad; how humans *use* that technology determines whether it becomes good or bad. Common-sense examples to help us understand this view include a hammer or morphine. Both can be used for good or for ill.

The second view is that technology, once developed, shapes our world and shapes us in particular ways. A piece of technology has power because of its design and purpose, and that power changes the way people interact with it and with each other. This view suggests that technology is not neutral. Common-sense examples of this include the Internet and vaccines. It is easy to see how both these technologies shape our world.

Whichever view we hold, as we enter an era of intensified tech, it will be increasingly important for people—especially Christians—to acknowledge that we *do* have a say in how we use technology, and even how others use technology in ways that affect us. It is too easy to blame technology for our problems rather than admitting that the problem lies within us.

In fact, if we do not own our responsibility with the use of technology, we have relinquished power—not to technology itself, but to culture and the ideologies carried along with new technologies.

NEXT STOP: TOMORROWLAND

In the end, the relationship between God, people, and technology is complex, and it is not getting any simpler. Rather than pick some technology and debate its merits or demerits, *Braving the Future* tries to explain how these three things—God, people, technology—interrelate, so that we can understand how to respond to new technologies on the near horizon.

Our future is one in which rapid technological change will occur. Short of a worldwide cataclysm, or God deciding to call it a day and wrapping everything up, technological advance is inevitable. This doesn't mean there won't be skirmishes around the release of certain technologies. Killer robots, invasive drones, and robot companions: these are among technologies on the horizon that many people will come together to prevent. People of faith should indeed question and even stand against some future technologies. But calling Christians to action around specific technologies is not the primary task of this book. Taking stands against individual technologies is a difficult issue best worked out in church communities and within individual consciences. There is not always a clear answer—just look at the use of DDT to combat malaria and the production of genetically modified crops for hungry populations. Rather, we will consider together the larger questions about how to follow Christ in this new world of limitless tech.

What we will find, if we can get below the surface, is that technology is adopted through culture, and that this culture shapes how we use technology, which shapes how we see ourselves and how we see God. In this book, we are going to reverse engineer that process to see how a God-informed view of technology can better shape people. This reverse-engineered process will also help us to respond appropriately to any culture that tries to sneak in through new technology without dismissing the technology itself.

In this book, we're going to look at eight key technologies that will shape our future: virtual reality, autonomous machines, gene editing, artificial intelligence, brain-computer interfaces, intelligent robots, nanotechnology, and cybernetics. We'll approach these techs in this order since this represents a likely progression of cultural impact over the twenty-first century. We're going to look at each with an eye to popular culture by opening with a recent movie illustration. Each of the movies was selected purposefully; if you haven't seen them, watch them with an eye to the way they treat coming tech. Last, we'll tease out the underlying assumptions that these technologies will bring. The focus of our discussion is not the technologies themselves but *the assumptions behind them*. Once we have those assumptions in hand, we will apply each one to what we already know to be true about God and people. Hopefully this approach will help us be prepared to address the use of new tech even as it emerges.

Human nature encourages us to pick a side and become simplistic and even dualistic on the issue. Some hear about bad uses of tech and say, "See? It really is from the devil!" I think I can speak for myself and most people reading this book when I say that we've all been tempted to feel that way about some use of tech. On the other hand, we might be convinced by pragmatism to the extent that we're enthralled by the use of every new technology.

I use the phrase *use of tech* because, while we may not be able to stop the creation of tech—and I personally don't want to—in most situations, we can choose how we use it. In all situations, we can speak up to help society determine the best use of tech. If we just see tech as inherently bad, we become tech pessimists.

When I talk tech, people often peg me as a tech optimist. But when they use the word *optimist*, they suggest that I "believe" in all tech. It's like the only options are to subscribe to either Wendell Berry (an environmental activist and cultural critic) or Ray Kurzweil (a computer scientist and inventor), with nothing in between. This clouds the issues. One can be optimistic (as I am), without being naïve (which I hope I am not). Likewise, one can be cautious about tech (more cautious than I am, for example) without being pessimistic. I find that naïveté and pessimism are both unfruitful when it comes to tech. They are the extremes—we want to be in the middle. Color me optimistic, if a little cautious.

If you know a little about technology and are hesitant about what lies on the horizon, then this book is for you. *Braving the Future* will help you think through how tech shapes our lives and our world and will help you hold onto hope in God's provision in the midst of what may seem to you like frightening days ahead. If you are tech savvy and excited about the potential of emerging technologies, this book is also for you. *Braving the Future* will assist you to think critically about the tech that you have and are planning to embrace.

Often, when it comes to issues related to science and technology, Christian discussions seem about two steps behind. Here, in these pages, we're trying to move one step ahead.

Ready to brave the future? If so, please keep your hands and arms inside the vehicle and remain seated at all times. Hang on to your personal belongings, 'cause here we go!

ONE

READY PLAYER ONE
VIRTUAL REALITY AND THE
ADDICTION OF TECH

*Before long, billions of people around the world were working
and playing in the OASIS every day. Some of them met, fell in
love, and got married without ever setting foot on the same con-
tinent. The lines of distinction between a person's real identity
and that of their avatar began to blur. It was the dawn of a new
era, one where most of the human race now spent all of their
free time inside a videogame.*
—ERNEST CLINE, *READY PLAYER ONE*

When Wade Watts enters the OASIS, Wade ends and Parzival begins. In the real world, Wade is a nerdy eighteen-
year-old from The Stacks, a piled-up, mega-sized trailer park
in Oklahoma City. But in the OASIS, a multiplayer online
game, Parzival is a *gunter* (aka "Egg hunter"), who spends
his time questing for a hidden Easter Egg that will reward its
finder with control over the OASIS. If you met Wade in the
real world and Parzival in the OASIS, you would notice that

Parzival looks a bit like Wade—or at least an idealized form of Wade. The acne is gone, but the face and body styles are close, or close enough. With as much time as Wade spends in the OASIS, it begs the question: who is more real—Wade or Parzival?

No one in the OASIS will ever know what a player's real-world form looks like unless the player allows it. In the OASIS, a player chooses how they will appear to others by creating an avatar, or representation, of themselves. In creating their avatar, the player can be whoever they want to be: they can be black, they can be white, they can be green, they can be fuchsia, they can be male, they can be female, they can be intersex, they can be nonbinary, they can be human, they can be minotaur, they can be Care Bear™. With the amount of time people like Wade spend in the OASIS, this is more than mere aesthetics of avatar design.[1] A person in the OASIS can go anywhere and do anything. The virtual sky—sometimes red, sometimes blue—is the limit. Parzival may not be a gangly, purple-skinned Cyclops dressed in a muumuu with a magic glow stick, but he's probably met one somewhere along the way.

Such is the world of *Ready Player One*, the film by Stephen Spielberg based on the book by Ernest Cline.[2] *Ready Player One* depicts the year 2045, a future wherein a sprawling multiverse of virtual worlds—the OASIS—has enraptured the world. Billions of people spend as many of their waking hours as possible living in the OASIS, connected via their virtual reality visors and their haptic gloves. Wade, the main character, has named his avatar Parzival in honor of Sir Percival, one of the Knights of the Round Table who quested for the Holy Grail, just as Parzival quests for the hidden Easter Egg placed in the OASIS world by its designer, James Halliday. Parzival's quest brings meaning to Wade's life. Though Parzival chooses to quest for something meaningful (more meaningful than, say, killing thousands of low-level kobolds for copper pieces), most of the other billion people in the OASIS are questing for . . . what? In this slightly dystopic view of the future, billions of people spend their lives in virtual reality, simply escaping the "real" reality outside their visors.

But if their real world is so inferior to their virtual world, can we blame them? Is it wrong to spend time in virtual reality? Is it wrong to spend your life in virtual reality?

What if everyone else was spending their lives in the virtual world—would you adapt to it too? What if you had a friend who felt called to be a missionary in the OASIS—would it be wrong then?

SAMPLE TECH: VIRTUAL REALITY

Virtual reality creates a fully immersive experience for the user by using the senses of sight, sound, and touch. Think of it as a technology that combines the power of the television, the internet, and the smartphone in one device and then amplifies this power. When a person enters a virtual world through a virtual reality device, the computer simulates an environment that the person's senses then confirm. Futurists believe that virtual reality is one of the next big things in tech evolution.[3] Far more than its predecessors—including internet chat rooms and social media—virtual reality will transform the way we communicate.

Here in the first half of the twenty-first century, virtual reality is on the verge of rapid adoption. Virtual worlds such as Second Life that came online in the first decade of the twenty-first century captured the attention of millions, but their impact on the world at large was limited. In part, this was because the technology had not yet matured; the experience was neither immersive (it was depicted in low-resolution 2D on a small flat screen), nor responsive (the only two senses engaged were sight and sound, with sound limited to that which emerged from computer speakers; there was no touch, taste, or smell). As a result, many people tend to lump virtual reality in with flying cars—a promised technology that hasn't delivered.

This judgment, however, is probably premature. Most major tech companies that are household names—Google, Apple, Amazon, Microsoft, Facebook—are investing significant resources in virtual reality. Each hopes to be the company that finally triggers widespread adoption.

When it arrives to the masses, virtual reality, just as the smartphone before it, will bring great advantages. For example, I think of my own occupation as a professor who teaches biblical subjects. Frequently when I cover a subject like the preaching and communication strategies of the earliest Christians, I describe to my students what it was like to be an apostle who used oral rhetoric in a synagogue or an outdoor marketplace. For my current students, the best I can reasonably do is try to create descriptions with my words and show some pictures of archeological ruins. In a few situations, there are CGI (computer-generated imagery) reconstructions of ancient places, but these tend to be limited and are still 2D.

I look forward to the day when my students and I will don visors and walk together in an ancient marketplace, hearing the text of the New Testament come alive amid the dust and dung. Even better, my online students will be able to join us in this virtual classroom, such that the disadvantages that online students face today will largely vanish. We will all virtually go to the courtyard of the Jerusalem temple to see the money-changers and temple patrons in action.

With the rewards of virtual reality, however, come increased risks. Right now, when we communicate with others online, the worst behavior we typically encounter is an ugly tweet or blog comment. This type of negative feedback can range from the annoying to the depressing to the infuriating. Because technology amplifies usage, virtual reality will increase the ability of abusers to exploit far more than they can now. Worse than the nameless Sixers that Parzival fought in *Ready Player One*, these abusers will give new meaning to the term *trolls*. One day we may be traveling the virtual world, trying to make it to a doctor's appointment on time, only to get held up by an ugly green-skinned monster.

There is one reason that people will adopt virtual reality without pause: it will increase interconnectivity.[4] The telegraph, telephone, email, and social media became indispensable parts of our culture because they connected people. These technologies offer "intimacy," suggests *WIRED* editor Peter Rubin, which is why they are so powerful.[5] At first blush, *intimacy* may sound like the wrong word, but each of these previous iterations of connective technologies do produce intimacy.

As a teenager, I spent an inordinate amount of time talking to my closest friends Ken and Bubba on the telephone. This created intimacy, though of a different sort than the kind we experience when we meet others in person or through social media. Even social media creates intimacy, though the technology limits and colors that intimacy. Think of it like this: The telegraph created a sort of intimacy, but nothing compared to its successor, the telephone. The telegraph is to the telephone what social media will be to virtual reality. Can you imagine what it was like before the telephone? I can't. And people born late in the twenty-first century will never be able to understand what it was like before virtual reality. It's that much of a game-changer.

I WANT A NEW DRUG

The evolution of technology shows no signs of abating. We are at a place in history in which, if futurists are correct, tech will only increase its scope and power to change our lives. This will also trigger a related effect: its speed of adoption by consumers. Once the telegraph proved so useful, consumers were quick to want the telephone. Now that social media has proven so useful, consumers will be quick to want the more immersive virtual world (once it reaches the requisite critical mass of adopters and content).

This acceleration of creation and adoption makes it a challenge for Christians to formulate thoughtful and wise responses to technology. It also makes for an unsettling feeling when new tech arrives. This is because once new technology begins to be adopted, it also becomes addictive.[6] When I use the word *addictive* to describe our relationship with technology, I don't mean the word in the clinical sense—though that usage is appropriate in certain circumstances. Instead, I mean it in the everyday sense of a strong desire: "Wow, that dark chocolate brownie was so addictive!"

The advent of the smartphone in the past decade shows just how addictive technology can be. We've all been in public places where scores of people sat glued to their phones. And we have seen people using their phones while trying to walk down the street, bumping into things as they go (which would appear to be a sure sign of the zombie apocalypse). Our smartphones are so vital a part of our daily lives that we cannot keep our hands off them. One study of smartphone use found that the average smartphone user touched their phone about 164 times an hour. That's 2,617 times a day—more if you sleeptext.

Let's put this in perspective.

Common Human Activities—Number per Day[7]

Heart Beat	100,800
Take Breath	23,040
Touch Smartphone	2,617
Touch Face	376
Wash Hands	8

Every day we touch our iPhones 300 times more than we wash our hands. Ewww! Not only is that a lot of germs on our phones—sparking magazine articles with headlines such as "Your Cell Phone Is 10 Times Dirtier Than a Toilet Seat"—it is also a lot of addiction.[8] This level of addiction, which comes via a marvel of a tech that has changed our world, explains why tech philosophers sometimes speak of new technology as an extension of ourselves. Considering the rate we interact with our phones, they are almost like parts of ourselves.

There are other ways in which technology is extremely addictive. Let's consider another (and less germy) marvel of modern tech: high definition television (HDTV). Today HDTV is the standard. Many people now have 4K and even 8K televisions (with 4,000 or 8,000 pixels of resolution), but almost no one still uses low-resolution TVs. Yet I, and maybe some readers of this book, grew up with low-resolution TVs. I spent many Sunday afternoons after church at my Mom-Mom's house, watching reruns of classic shows on a 27-inch color TV. That was great then. But there is no way that I would now watch *Avengers: Infinity War* on that kind of television. Ever. As tech improves, we become addicted to the new standards that tech offers, and it becomes hard to go back to old technology. Sure, someone somewhere may like to visit his barber for a seasonal bloodletting or be interested in copper piping for the water lines of her new home. But let's agree: not many.

Our need for tech is so highly addictive that we can liken technology to a drug. This drug is really not a new drug—it has always been the case that new technology is addictive. I can assure you that three thousand years ago, the first time an Egyptian pharaoh saw an enemy on the battlefield use a chariot, that Egyptian pharaoh had to have one. And once he got one, he never went into battle without it again. He became addicted to the chariot because of the strategic advantages it offered.

From the beginning of recorded history until the late nineteenth century, it is unlikely anyone would have spoken of technology as "addictive." Up until that point, tech progress was slow enough that new technologies only appeared once in a person's lifetime. As the pace of progress quickens, however, and the faster new inventions become a reality, the more addictive tech feels. And all this acceleration just feeds our addiction. This is why I can assure you that next week, the first time a CEO sees his corporate enemy flying in first class use the newest eThingamajig, that CEO will have to have one. And once he gets it, he'll never go into the boardroom without it—well, at least until the next technology comes along. More and more tech, more and more frequently, at lower and lower costs, feeds our addiction.

IF WE MAKE IT, THEY WILL USE IT

Our addiction to new tech will ensure that corporations will continue to produce it. In general, the creation of new technology is a good thing. Most new technologies have the ability to make our lives better. But not all new tech actually does. Some emerging tech, such as genetically modified viruses, can be quite dangerous to people in many scenarios. And some new tech, such as Snapchat, can seem useful at first but then quickly take a wrong turn, to the point that it probably does more harm than good. And then there is new tech that has not arrived yet—like the de-extinction of saber-tooth tigers—that seems like a bad idea to even pursue.

So how can we tell what kind of tech is good and what kind is bad? How can we make sure we do not use bad tech, or use good tech badly?

As I mentioned in the introduction, we can think about technology and its relationship to our world in several different ways. Two of the most prominent views are known as instrumentalism and determinism. We can think of these two views as being on two ends of a spectrum.

tech is a tool	tech is a world-shaper
← ■ ■ ▪ ▪ ▪ ▪ ׀ ׀ ▪ ▪ ▪ ■ ■ →	
human power > tech power	human power < tech power

Instrumentalism is the view that technology is merely a tool that people can use (or not), and the belief that its effects are limited by use. Determinism, on the other end of the spectrum, sees technology as an active agent that forms culture, molds human choice and interaction, and shapes the future.[9] As you move left on this continuum, you view power over tech as resting more in the hands of people than in those of technology. As you move to the right, you view technology as holding the upper hand, exerting control over individuals and culture. Again, there are other views than these, but these are the predominant perspectives.

Before we jump to social media, self-driving cars, or Terminator-type cyborgs—the current low-hanging fruit of technological criticism—let's go back a few years. One of the greatest technologies ever invented was the composite bow. The adoption of this technology is lost to history, but it occurred sometime before the seventeenth century BC.[10] Unlike the standard or "self-bow," the composite bow was made of materials working together that allowed a recurve form. This meant it was small, flexible, and extremely powerful, and made it possible for people to shoot on horseback and to create whole new battle tactics, such as the Parthian shot.[11] Was this technology a tool that did a job at the behest of people, as instrumentalism would suggest? Or were these terrifying new weapons world-shapers, as determinism would maintain—things that, once used, altered the balance of power in the ancient world?

Another one of the greatest technologies ever invented resulted from the vision of Prince Henry at the beginning of the fifteenth century, in the small country of Portugal. This tech, called the caravel, was a sailing ship that improved so much on previous vessels that it could efficiently explore whole oceans, not just seas. It sailed fast with a reduced crew. The creation of the caravel meant the entire world was now accessible by sea.[12] Without the caravel, Columbus would never have sailed the ocean blue. Again, we ask the question: Was the caravel a simple tool for crossing oceans? Or was it a world-shaper that, once deployed, would have no choice but to change the course of history?

Many readers will read these examples and say, "Well, both!" It is indeed tempting to choose both—many philosophers of technology also try to do this, locating themselves somewhere between instrumentalism and determinism. At the end of the day, however, there is a choice to make, a question to answer. Do a composite bow, a caravel, Gutenberg's printing press, and my Wii each have their own agency or not? If you think that my Wii has its own will, and shapes the world through its will, then you lean toward determinism. (My kids must be determinists, as they would love to claim that their videogames *make* them keep playing past their daily limit.) But if you believe that my Wii does not have agency and its effects depend on how we use it, then you lean toward instrumentalism.

But—I hear your protest coming—the Wii is just a videogame console; it clearly does not impact world history in the same way as a composite bow or the caravel. Yet all three of these examples are technologies that are either tools or agents. I admit, it's difficult. When we're talking caravels and social media, we are ready to speak of the dark forces of tech agency. But when we're talking Wiis and socket wrenches, we may feel better claiming that technologies are really just tools to use or not.

Many Christian thinkers today lean toward determinism— the belief that tech has agency and wields preferences in our world. But the truth is this: tech is really more of a tool—or, if you prefer, a tool with consequences.[13] When we create tech, that tech does not affect anything until we use it. The agency of the technology comes not from within tech itself but from the humans who put it to use.[14] It is true that using tech—such as the caravel or the printing press—can create immeasurable consequences, which can reverberate through history. This does not change the fact that it was people who put the tech into play.

This argument is especially difficult when applied to tech seemingly created only for evil. It can be hard to see anti-personnel mines and mustard gas as neutral, having neither good nor bad purposes. Even these extreme examples of bad tech, however, do not escape the human agency behind their use. People may have created these technologies, but people may also put them aside. Most countries in our world have outlawed mustard gas and no longer produce antipersonnel mines.

One reason why I favor the instrumental view is that it puts the responsibility of use squarely in the laps of people. There is another reason: it encourages people to be discerning about what tech they should use, and how and when and where they should use it. If we believe that tech has its own agency, we can begin to think we are off the hook, because there is nothing we can do. It can lead to rejection and disassociation of tech and culture rather than engagement. People should instead actively think and pray about the tech they bring into their lives. Only then can we best discern how God wants to use tech in our world.

No technology is unstoppable. Think way back to 2013, when Google launched its ambitious Google Glass (the creepy eyeglasses that among other things allowed people to walk around videoing everyone). The advent of that new technology was met with disdain. It was mocked on late night TV, and the average person voiced major privacy concerns. Eventually Glass wearers were expelled from restaurants and other public places.[15] Though Google Glass is still for sale as of this writing, it will never be accepted in its current form in U.S. and Canadian culture. People stopped the use of this technology. Likewise, governments, corporations, and nonprofits can also deter technology when they put their collective minds to it. We may not be able to stop the creation of tech that people will use poorly or for evil. But we can stand against it.[16]

If you are reading this book, you are a tech user. Paperback books with covers and acid-free paper and ebooks on a Kindle are both forms of modern tech. You and I are called to live in such a way that our technology helps us be devoted to God and love others as we love ourselves (see Matthew 22:37-40). If any tech in our lives is preventing us from doing those two things, then that tech needs to go the way of Google Glass.

YOU CAN GO YOUR OWN WAY

The siren song of technologies such as virtual reality is the ability to do whatever a person can imagine. When we use virtual reality (VR), it quickly gives us the impression that we can shape our own reality. And in one sense, that is exactly what happens. When we enter a virtual world, we shed any limitations exerted by the real world and we feel limitless in our options or abilities. In the real world, I cannot stand on top of Mount Everest or Olympus Mons, but I can in virtual reality. In the real world, I cannot fly (aside from planes or ultralights), but I can in virtual reality. In the real world, I cannot turn my forearm into a broadsword, but I can in virtual reality. In the real world, I cannot do ugly things to people without consequences, but I can in virtual reality. There are limits in VR, but the limits are only those placed by the designer of the virtual world. And as we have seen through several Silicon Valley scandals, the designers of our virtual reality future probably look less like the benevolent James Halliday and more like the nefarious IOI corporation of *Ready Player One*.

Let's balance out this discussion. Even in the real world, we who are privileged with resources and choices create our own reality every day. Each day when we wake up, we act like Sims, constructing our own realities: we choose what we will wear, what our activities will be, and what stories we will tell others about ourselves. This creation of reality is easy to spot on social media; many Facebook profiles contain weekly posts of smiling, happy families engaged in their latest, greatest adventure. Behind those photos, of course, are average people who struggle with their jobs, their marriages, and their kids. But social media gives them the power to define their reality.

The desire to define reality has been a hallmark of humanity from the beginning. In medieval Europe, a peasant could travel by oxcart to a new village, change his name, and create a new reality. Because communication was poor, and not too many people cared about peasants, he was likely successful in his attempt to start over. However, in many ways, the peasant's new reality was not that different from his old reality. Though his name and story changed, his living conditions generally remained the same. This became less true once we reached the modern era; by this point people could immigrate via steamship from country to country. They could change not only their names and their stories, but also, in some cases, their living conditions in dramatic ways. The greater the range of technology, the more people seem able to alter their reality.[17] Ultimately, people want the ability to create their own lives and make their own decisions and be unhampered by anything outside of their control.

The greater the technology, the more we feel we have the power to do what we want. Today, each generation sets a new meaning for the phrase "the sky's the limit." Tomorrow, we might strap on our virtual reality visors and haptic suits and realize even the sky is no longer the limit—because there is no sky unless we create one.

With each advance in technology comes an increasing risk of the assumption of human aseity. *Aseity* is a word that we use to describe God that basically means "self-sufficient" or "self-reliant." In other words, the more powerful technology becomes, the more it will tempt people to believe that they are self-sufficient or autonomous. In fact, it's not only tech itself that is highly addictive; it's also the feeling that we are all that matters.

Future technologies like virtual reality may prove to be so addictive that our lives in tech begin to define our existence. In *Ready Player One*, all of Wade Watt's existence outside of virtual reality was an annoyance; therefore, he lived most of his life as Parzival within virtual reality. There he (Parzival) was completely self-reliant. We can become more our VR selves than is good, just as Wade was perhaps more Parzival than was healthy. Even if we as individuals never enter a virtual world, tech advances will still suggest that we are our own self-contained islands. When I can buy a house, and then work online, attend virtual church, have robots do my chores and drones deliver my groceries, I will never have to interact with any other people.

ASEITY

Our belief that we are self-reliant—or that we can ever be
self-reliant—is a myth. Aseity, or self-existence, is a property
of God, not of people. As the theologian William Lane Craig
explains, "God is not dependent upon any other being for His
existence; rather, He exists independently of everything else."[18]
Tech gives us the impression that we are all we need. But unlike
God, people *do* lack. We do have needs. Whatever needs we as
people have, we will try to fill them. If we fill that lack with the
wrong things, we will end up in the wrong places.

As new tech appears on the horizon, people will begin to
adopt it, and soon it will be addictive to everyone exposed
to it. Yet it is still our responsibility to determine how much
we use any new tech and to what degree. Let's look at an
example: By the end of the twenty-first century, dermal
regenerators will likely be commonplace medical devices. If
I cut my hand slicing kiwis (because I went "old school" and
fixed a fruit salad myself instead of just letting my house
robot do it), I can use this miracle of modern technology to
heal the cut on my hand and get right back to slicing kiwis.
That's all well and good. At the same time, a dermal regenerator implies that I don't need to worry too much about my
external body health. In the future, if someone challenges
me to a game of knives and I lose and stick my hand with a
knife, it will hurt for a few moments—until the regenerator
starts to work. Today, I would never play that game, because
I take the health of my hands and the risk of injuring them
more seriously.

It may be hard to relate to this example. But I suggest the
same thing is already occurring today with our use of pharma-
ceuticals. These pills are new tech, having existed for only a

few short decades. But already we treat our bodies differently today than people did a century ago. We are more aware of what drugs can help with (and what they can't). We can, and do, because we know that many ailments (especially pain) are readily curable by the right drug.

Neither dermal regenerators nor pharmaceutical drugs necessarily promote a false sense of aseity in our hearts. For the most part, these items are tools; if we use them well, they will bring good into our lives. Yet culture is quick to promote a false sense of aseity through the use of these tools. A hundred years ago, if I had a headache that wouldn't go away, my Christian friends would undoubtedly pray for me if I asked. Today I likely would not think to ask them to pray; I would just go take a couple of Tylenol. From Tylenol to dermal regenerators, from virtual reality to salt water pools, each new invention in our lives is an excuse for culture to whisper in our hearts, "You've got everything you need."

Culture will also promote transhumanist ideas—those which bring with them a spirit of aseity. The idea behind transhumanism is more than simply for us to advance in our abilities to shape the world; the goal is to redefine what it means to be human. Transhumanism suggests that we are all that matters in our universe, and that we must evolve to the next phase of human existence so that we can be truly self-reliant. We leave our mortal limitations behind, becoming something closer to divine. The more transhuman we become, the less we need to rely on outmoded ideas about God. In fact, tech accelerates this idea. Each new gadget we acquire creates an "enchantment" for us that makes us seem as though we are all that matter in our world.[19]

Above I noted that the siren song of virtual reality and related technologies is that they are quick to make us believe we can do whatever we want, be whoever we want to be. Practically speaking, no tech can actually erase our needs and inadequacies. More importantly, no tech can overturn the theological truth that we are created beings, and that as created beings, we will always need things from our Creator. The more we believe we can do whatever we want, the more we impinge on God's space.

God created people with certain parameters that are essential to not only our existence but also to our wholeness. For example, one parameter God created was our life span. This means that people come into life and then, at some point in time, exit life. This parameter is essential because we can't change it (even if we are successful at extending it). Another parameter that God created was an expectation that we would love each other and live at peace with one another. That is pretty hard to do when we become convinced by tech that we are all independent island nations.

FLOATING TECH

One of the most amazing stories in the Bible takes place in 2 Kings 6:1–7. It includes God, people, tech, and the miraculous. In this story, a company of prophets comes to Elisha and asks him if they can set up a new headquarters by the Jordan River, as where they had been meeting with him was too small. Elisha agrees and even goes along with them after another prophet asks him to accompany them.

Once at the Jordan, the band of prophets starts to fell trees to make their new meeting place. As one of the unnamed prophets is chopping, the head of the prophet's axe flies off the handle and into the river. The prophet calls for Elisha to do something, as the axe is a borrowed one. Upon learning where the axe head fell into the water, Elisha cuts a stick and throws it into the water, and the axe head floats to the surface! Following Elisha's instructions, the prophet retrieves the head of his borrowed axe.

The story of Elisha is set at the end of the ninth century BC, or in the midst of the second Iron Age. The Bible describes the axe head that is lost in the river as made of iron, which was a relatively new technology at that time. Based upon several clues in the story, the axe head must have been an expensive tool loaned to this prophet and not something the owner would want to lose. We know from archaeology that these axe heads had a pocket in them that held the wooden haft. This generally worked well, although mishaps with axe heads were probably common.

What happens next is lost to history. For reasons unknown to us today, when Elisha sees the prophet's distress, he cuts a stick and throws it in the water. There must be some cultural or scientific logic to Elisha's actions (similar to Jesus spitting and using saliva to heal a deaf and mute man; see Mark 7:33-34). Based on the faith of Elisha and the prophet, and signified by the action of throwing the stick in the water, God does the miraculous and causes the axe head to float so that the prophet may retrieve it.

What is the point of this story? Surely more tools were lost in Elisha's day than just this one. Yet given the extremely limited number of stories the Bible records over its millennia of coverage, every story the Bible includes is there for a very specific reason. We can safely assume that it wasn't because God cared about new human technology. What we can say is that this miracle ties in with the relationship God has with people.

Unlike God, we are not self-sufficient. That axe head was an expensive tool for which the prophet was responsible. Its loss would have carried significant consequences. The prophet needed help, and his community (in the person of Elisha) and his Creator (God) both responded. Admitting we need help is part of truly seeing who we are for who we are and recognizing our own insufficiency. Recognizing our own limits is a powerful counter to the myth of human aseity or autonomy. The apostle Paul writes that in Christ—not in humans—"all things hold together" (Colossians 1:17). Through Christ, lost things are found and wholeness is restored.

In *Ready Player One*, the people in the OASIS never worry about lost axe heads. Whatever they lose, they can easily regain. They don't see themselves for who they are. These kinds of technologies are exciting, but they convey a false sense of our place in the world. We are not self-sufficient. We need God even in the small things, even though we don't always understand the whys or the hows.

God not only floats axe heads—God floats our very lives.

REAL STEEL
AUTONOMOUS MACHINES
AND HAPPINESS

Behind the handlers is Colossus himself, much taller and broader than the robots we've seen. He towers over Max as he struts by. He has a platinum silver sheen that covers his long arms and legs. There is a modern sleekness to Colossus. You have never seen a machine so sophisticated in your life.

—JEREMY LEVEN AND JOHN GATINS, *REAL STEEL*

Nothing in the world is as electrifying as robot boxing. I still remember the night Max Kenton entered Virgin America Motor City Spectrum in Detroit, followed closely by Atom. Max had turned on Atom's shadow function, which allowed the eight-foot robot to mimic precisely the eleven-year-old boy's actions. I'm not sure where Max's showmanship came from, but when the crowd saw him—and the robot behind him—start to dance, it set the crowd on fire. By now, people were used to seeing robots move by themselves, with some instructions from their human controllers. But there was something about the robot Atom dancing his way to the fight against Twin Cities that night—something graceful that was beyond mere robot. It was more "human" than any-thing I had seen before. It was, in a sense, "real steel."

The year 2020 was a milestone for the sports world, as human prize fighting became illegal and human boxers were replaced with robots. In this newest version of box-ing, robot fighters are king. These robots can dish out more abuse, and take more abuse, than we ever thought possible. We can make them do things a human fighter would never do. These robots are physically impressive, but they are not intelligent; they still need directions from people. Yet they can do a lot with just minimal instructions or training. The balance between machine movement and human intelli-gence makes robot boxing truly exciting.

This vision of the near future is from Shawn Levy's film *Real Steel*.[1] In the near future, humanity will start to rely on machines to do things that humans can't or won't do any longer. This vision is not far from reality; we already have machines on assembly lines and robots poised to break into service in retail locations such as fast food.[2] The world of *Real Steel* is on our doorstep.

While we may not have robot boxers in 2020, we will see automation occupy a growing place of importance in our world. From bricklaying robots to self-driving cars, the twenty-first century looks primed for a robot revolution. What could be wrong with that? Well, just the idea of self-driving cars has many people concerned.

Are there any limits to which we should not allow auto-mation to take over our lives? Is there anything that people should do even if machines can? What if the machine is argu-ably better at it? What will we lose if many things we do today are soon replaced by automation?

SAMPLE TECH: AUTONOMOUS MACHINES

A machine is any device that helps people do work. People have used machines since early in recorded history, when new advances in technology led to machines such as the screw (third century BC) and the iron plow (first century AD). Each of these machines have had an incalculable impact on human civilization since their adoption. Up until the end of the twentieth century, however, virtually all machines accomplished work only in combination with human effort. For example, the steam locomotive may be a complex machine, but it won't go anywhere without a human engineer. These kinds of simple machines helped humans do work, but they did not do work without humans. With the advent of machine learning, we are now on the cusp of a revolution in machine technology: the autonomous machine.

An autonomous machine is any device that helps people do work by doing the work itself. These types of machines do not need constant tending by humans. They can keep working and accomplishing their tasks long after the human has left the building. Whereas unintelligent machines can assist us in achieving linear growth in our accomplishments, autonomous machines can help us achieve exponential growth. We are on the cusp of a revolution because of this fact: what actually held machines back from doing more work was us.

Today, we already have autonomous machines in service around us. In fact, whether we like it or not, we are already putting our lives in the hands of automated machines. Modern jumbo jets are mostly autonomous, in that all but seven minutes of a flight are typically under the control of the autopilot.[3] We are already accustomed to automation in factories and in larger commercial endeavors, but where the revolution will occur is in the increase of autonomous machines in our every-day lives. Think Roomba but not limited to merely vacuuming.

A couple of years ago, I was walking along the street that runs parallel to the beach in Cervia, Italy. Only a line of high-rise hotels separated me from the waters of the Adriatic. As I walked, I casually looked into each manicured courtyard of the upmarket hotels. As I passed by courtyard after courtyard, one caused me to stop and do a double take. Peering through the black, wrought-iron fence, I saw a nondescript metal rect-angle the size of a large cardboard box zipping backward and forward over the small front lawn. At first I didn't understand what I was looking at. Within a minute, it dawned on me what it was: an autonomous lawnmower. In the next minute, I wondered why I hadn't yet seen one back home in the United States. In the third minute, I wondered how long it would take before I could get one for my own yard. I could imagine it very well: sitting in my oversized white Adirondack chair with blue and green cushions on a hot summer day, sipping a cold drink while our lawn Roomba speeds by and does its job. Now *that*, I imagine, is what it will mean to "cut the grass" in the mid-twenty-first century.

The beauty of autonomy is that we will soon be able to add it to almost any type of machine that exists. If you come to my house, you will see I own an automatic espresso machine (I know, I know; it's not a real espresso machine). *Automatic* means I don't have to grind the beans or blend the water, but also that I still have to do everything else: turn it on, wait for it to heat up, place a cup, wait for it to distill the espresso, and then mix in the chocolate, coconut water, and milk. What I look forward to is an autonomous espresso machine: when the machine learns from my smartphone that I have awoken, it will get to work and have my wake-up concoction ready to go by the time I arrive in the kitchen. Not much intelligence is needed here beyond what is already feasible by today's technology. We'll look at this in a later chapter, but I tend to think of machines this way:

$$\text{automatic} \rightarrow \text{autonomous} \rightarrow \text{intelligent}$$

Once autonomous machines arrive in full force, they will bring greater benefits to our lives than merely autonomously made expressos and effortlessly mowed lawns. Self-driving cars are regularly cited as the next big autonomous machine, and I for one am (cautiously) excited about all the lifestyle improvements they will bring. I still remember being made to watch all those drunk-driving videos as a junior high student, so I know the death toll on U.S. highways is way too high (incredibly, there were 10,497 fatalities due to drunk driving in 2016).[4] Eradicating this scourge through autonomy will literally change our civilization overnight. It doesn't end there, of course; eliminating the stress of a morning and evening commute would make the quality of our lives so much better. Instead of falling into road rage because three cars try to slip through a now-red light in the left turn lane, I could peacefully read my notes for the day's meeting or catch up on my digital scrapbooking.

Two of the most commonly cited drawbacks to more autonomous machines are decreases in individual decision-making and the challenges of making these machines foolproof. Much of the relevance of the first criticism lies in how we perceive the world, and when we want machine exactitude versus human imperfection. For me, having autonomous lawnmowers will be great, because I want my grass to be cut as perfectly as possible. At the same time, I have concerns about a machine fetching my groceries based solely on bar-code recognition. Or a machine that paints the front door of my house a little too perfectly. These latter concerns tie into the problem of making these machines foolproof. Though autonomous machines will mess up less frequently than humans, when they do mess up, they will mess up big. The question then becomes "How do we use autonomous machines in ways that benefit, not hurt, our lives?"

WORK IN THE FUTURE

If cutting the grass soon goes the way of the dodo bird, what does this mean for the rest of our household chores? As a homeowner and father to four children who break things faster than I can fix them, I find that household chores take up a great deal of my spare time. It doesn't help that I am a recovering perfectionist, so I make sure these chores and repairs are done to some standard I set. In the near future, we will have access to more and more tools to help make our work go faster. From autonomous lawnmowers to intelligent ovens to 3D printers, we could assume that our future life will be full of leisure. But is this really true?

What will happen to human jobs once autonomous machines start to proliferate? We have seen robots replace the jobs of assembly line workers for the big automakers. At the same time, if we look back over the past several centuries, we see that the advancement of technology has not necessarily decreased our work if we only consider the big picture (in fact, in the United States, it may have increased it). Since economies are fluid and markets cyclical, autonomous machines don't mean there won't be periods of hardships; those are certain.

As I write, the United States is enjoying a lower unemployment rate than at any time during the Industrial Revolution. Instead of reducing our workload, what technology has done is change the way we work. Compared to a few centuries ago, the number of people who spend their lives farming has dramatically decreased, while the number of people who spend their lives in front of computers has dramatically increased. Work itself has not decreased; it's how we describe work that has changed. This is part of the reason work will always be a part of our lives. In this, futurists tend to agree that people will still work in the future; it's just that our work will be repurposed around new technology.[5]

Work is good. God created us with work in mind (see Genesis 2:15), and when we work it adds meaning and value to our lives (see Ecclesiastes 3:13). This is especially true if we broaden our definition of work a little. I was raised to believe work is labor that pays the bills and helps the next generation. Recent developments in theology, though, encourage us to have a more robust view of work. As Pope John Paul II famously said, "Work is for man, not man for work."[6] When we think of work, we can start from a more robust understanding:

- Work is not something that should be merely individual; work is something that should benefit those around us.
- Work is not something that we do because we have to; work is something that we should do in such a way that it allows us to use our God-given gifts.
- Work is not something that we should view as only fulfilling some original design from prehistory; work is something that should allow us to be a part of pointing toward the fulfillment of God's long-term plan in what we do.[7]

These enhanced ideas about work are both helpful and important. Yet I cannot help but think that our theology in this area has improved in small part because our technology improved. I am not suggesting that tech defines theology, but I am suggesting that tech assists us in making our lives better and that this includes even theology. Because of technology, our jobs are increasingly less about mere survival and more about helping our society. Even though these new ideas about work were just as true for Ancient Near Eastern laborers as they are for us today, it is hard to see how this view would have circulated in that environment.

In ages past, the difficulties of shaping the world around us meant that work defined us. In the future, we will define work. As more and more new tech arrives, more and more of our jobs will be in areas that benefit society and culture. Fewer and fewer people are forced to work in ways that they don't want to; we have so many rights and privileges compared to past generations. Tech has provided us with greater opportunities to see value in other people—a value that is in some ways flawed but in other ways mimics God's view of humanity.[8] In large part, we have technology to thank for this.

If this were all that tech did—help us to have more meaningful jobs that allow us to focus more on the betterment of our world—we would be in good shape. But there's another side to this aspect of work and tech—a darker one that our culture is quick to embrace.

THE LIMITS OF SATISFACTION

The future is not one long, idyllic vacation in which we will have plenty of downtime. This is good, as it will keep us working and keep us thinking about doing good for others and ourselves. Yet there is no doubt that as the nature of work changes, it will change our perceptions of work, our perceptions of ourselves, and how technology fits into that equation.

In the previous chapter, we discussed how addictive tech can be. Once I purchase and use an autonomous lawnmower, I will always need an autonomous lawnmower; there will be no going back to the way things were. There is another aspect of this phenomenon than mere addiction. Once I move to an autonomous lawnmower, I will never be able to go back to a regular lawnmower because the new tech has forever altered my perception of the way the world should be. If for some reason the robot breaks down and I am forced to mow my lawn by hand, I will be angry and resentful—even though I have mowed my lawn by hand many times before.

Why would doing work that I have done many times before make me angry and resentful? It's part of what Yuval Harari calls the "luxury trap." In *Sapiens*, he describes the trap this way: "One of history's few iron laws is that luxuries tend to become necessities and to spawn new obligations. Once people get used to a certain luxury, they take it for granted. Then they begin to count on it. Finally they reach a point where they can't live without it."[9]

Right now, I don't hate mowing the lawn, but I don't enjoy it either. Until recently I used an 80-volt rechargeable push mower as my primary mower, even though, at about an acre, my lot is a little large for that technology. The luxury of a whisper-quiet motor with fiddle-free maintenance is what influenced me to move from a gas mower to a battery-operated one. Still, it was the time factor that pushed me to finally buy a used riding gas mower to supplement my mowing—one that is extremely loud and has so far required a great deal of fuss and fiddling. Sometimes I spend more time fiddling with the riding mower that it takes me to hand-cut the lawn. It's frustrating.

A better way of saying it is that I am not—at all—content with my yard maintenance options. My wife is a saint who never says anything negative about the yard, but when the topic naturally arises, I am the first to use the seventeenth century as a defense: "If we lived in the 1600s, we wouldn't care one whit about the length of our grass." In other words, the luxury of owning an advanced technology—the lawnmower— has created an obligation that never existed before in history. (Note to teenaged readers: before you take this book to your parents as proof that your summer yardwork is a luxury, not an obligation, I have bad news for you. Because your parents adopted lawn tech, they have become addicted to lawn tech, meaning that their worldview now holds lawn tech as an obligation, not an option.)

In the seventeenth century, there was no technology—outside of domesticated sheep or hand scythes—that dealt with lawn maintenance. As a result, no one except the ultrawealthy thought much about lawn maintenance. In the eighteenth century, the nonwealthy started to pay more attention to sports, which brought more awareness of grass. Eventually, in 1830, Edwin Budding invented the first mechanical lawnmower. Today, if the iron-fisted reigns of many homeowners' associations are proof positive, people think a great deal about lawn maintenance. Especially those neighbors of yours who have too much time on their hands.

When it comes to lawns, many of us have fallen into the luxury trap. Today we live under the perception that we are obligated to manicure the grass that surrounds our houses. Worse, our neighbors also feel that we are obligated to manicure our lawns. To put it another way, we are not content with yards that would make Walt Whitman proud. The luxury of technology creates a spiritual problem for us.

Many Christians are familiar with Philippians 4:13, often quoted as "I can do all things through him who gives me strength." In U.S. pop culture, this verse is often taken to mean that God gives us the power to accomplish whatever we want to accomplish. But those pesky verse divisions (not part of the original letter to the Philippians) have misled us. If we go back and read the three verses that precede this statement, we note that it comes amid Paul's recollection of his personal experiences with the people in the church at Philippi:

> I rejoiced greatly in the Lord that at last you renewed your concern for me. Indeed, you were concerned, but you had no opportunity to show it. I am not saying this because I am in need, for I have learned to be content whatever the circumstances. I know what it is to be in need, and I know what it is to have plenty. I have learned the secret of being content in any and every situation, whether well fed or hungry, whether living in plenty or in want. (Philippians 4:10-12)

Thus, even though he has experienced the extremes in his life—both feast and famine—Paul has learned to be content. In fact, Paul teases, he has discovered the secret to being content in all circumstances: contentment with life is solely based on relationship with Christ.

How can this work in the twenty-first century? We are supposed to find our contentment in Christ, but the more tech that comes our way, the more opportunities there are to be discontented.

- Before the lawnmower, no one complained if the grass grew long.

- Before the candle, no one complained about not being able to read in the dark.
- Before the iron, no one complained about wrinkled clothes.
- Before the mobile phone, no one complained about always being available.
- Before HDTV, no one complained about low resolution.
- Before the autonomous espresso machine, no one complained about having to make their own espresso.

We are clearly inventing our way into discontentment!

By the mid to late twenty-first century, it's going to get worse. We will use 3D printing on demand, coupled with inexhaustible robot labor, to conjure up everything that we could ever imagine. In the end, we will never be satisfied; we will always want more. And yet the Bible warns that we are to "be content with what you have" (Hebrews 13:5). Jesus explains that while it is normal for us to have earthly needs, we cannot be like the rest of the world and chase after these things. We have to chase after God (see Matthew 6:30-33).

To me, this discussion makes me feel like life in a tech-saturated world is tantamount to being stuck in a 1980s video-game. We keep fighting the same battles over and over again, with little variation. Surely we were meant for more than this.

HAPPINESS, THE GOAL OF LIFE?

Being satisfied with what we have may be the secret to life, but what is the goal of life? Let's dismiss the easily dismissible: gaining wealth or fame, for example. Throughout the history of humanity, there is one goal that appears over and over again: happiness. Take as an example the United States

Declaration of Independence, which famously states that all people should have "life, liberty, and the pursuit of happiness." Since we hear that expression so many times, it is easy to give it little thought. But what does the Declaration mean by "happiness"? Based on pop culture, it is easy for us to think of happiness as an emotion, simple enough to be represented in our texts and emails with an emoji: ☺. But what if happiness is more than an emoji?

The idea that happiness is the goal of life goes back at least as far as Greek philosophy. Most major schools of Greek thought believed that the point of life was to achieve something they called *eudaimonia*. We can describe this idea as "happiness," but in the Declaration of Independence sense, not in the emoji sense. Another word that we could use to describe this idea would be *flourishing*. In the ancient Greek sense, the purpose of life was to achieve happiness in our lives by flourishing in them. Greek thinkers often pointed to living good lives and possessing virtue to achieve happiness. To put it another way, true happiness came through living a meaningful life, not through gaining emotional highs or spending time on self-pleasure.

I'm not convinced that happiness is the ultimate goal for life, though it is a positive aspect of the real goal of life that Christians can embrace. Instead, the goal of life is to be *blessed* by God (see Deuteronomy 2:7; Job 42:12; Ephesians 1:3). This is one reason why the word *blessing* appears descriptively (rather than in a guideline or calling) so many times in the Bible. It describes what our lives should look like if we are truly flourishing. In order to be happy or to flourish, you must be blessed. And blessing from God comes by being obedient (see Deuteronomy 11:26-28, 28:1-2; Psalm 112:1; Luke

11:28). Jesus gives examples of such blessing in his Sermon on the Mount (see Matthew 5:3-12).

The advance of technology means that the stakes have never been higher. When Greek philosophers argued for human flourishing, their limited access to technology meant that most of the people they knew never made it to what we consider today to be middle age. For them, life was very difficult, so one had to make of it what they could. In contrast, today most people in the West can easily be lulled into a false sense of happiness by our technological advancement. Our culture encourages us to pursue happiness for happiness's sake, and it now offers us tech to help achieve this happiness.[10] But this is tangential to a biblical view, which sees our commitment to God as the source of what makes life good.

The more tech we possess, the less it may seem we need to worry about possessing virtue. In ages past, people felt virtue could be built through hard work and difficult conditions. When I was entering high school, my mom made me get a summer job as a busboy at a local restaurant because "it was good for me." But in the future, when autonomous machines do all the hard work, how will we build virtue in ourselves and our children? If virtues such as prudence, courage, and fairness are developed through work, does a changing landscape of work mean a changing definition of virtue?

In *Real Steel*, there is one extended scene in which director Shawn Levy places the camera directly on the face of the robot Atom. The viewer is made to look into the silent, blank stare of an impassive robot from several different angles. I use the word *impassive* here to mean that the robot has no connection or emotional attachment to the world around it. Unlike robots, people are not typically impassive. However, when we are impassive—uncaring to each other and to our world—the results are devastating. Sci-fi writers and tech philosophers have long pointed out that there is a risk when both robots and people become impassive about each other.[11]

For Christians, the God we know and worship is not impassive. God cares about us on a deeper level than we can understand or appreciate. Though we may be comfortable with this idea, it is actually rather peculiar: That the God of the universe, whose ways are not our ways, is not detached from us. Humans are impassive about ants; why is God not impassive toward humans? And yet God is not impassive toward us in the least; God's love for us is immeasurable and intimate. In fact, God wants to bless us so we can live good lives.

God is not impassive, but God is impassible. Though these two words are related, they mean two different things. *Impassible* is a word that we use to describe God that basically means "unaffected by His creatures."[12] In other words, though God cares about people, people don't really have the power to change God's mind. We cannot get God to do something God doesn't necessarily want to do.

This is where the influence of culture on future tech will create challenges: The marketing and promotion of tech will tempt us to see ourselves as impassible in relation to the world around us. The more automated our lives become, the more our attitudes toward automation will entice us to believe that we are above all of it and unmoved by it (see Matthew 18:7). We will risk living increasingly unsatisfied lives in which technology drives selfish interests, because we will not see any of our actions as fundamentally selfish. This is the opposite of both virtue and blessing.

IMPASSIBILITY

When we try to understand who God is, we keep coming back to how God relates to people. Does God love people? Yes! God shows his great love for people in many ways. Two of the most significant are through God's creative and communicative actions with us. Yet God does not have a *need* for people the way people have a need for God. Even more than this, God is unaffected by the events of the world not because he chooses to be somehow distant but because the world is part of creation and God is uncreated. We as people are very much affected by the world around us.

God's impassible nature is not an easy one to understand. As theologian J.I. Packer explains, the impassibility of God

> represents no single biblical term, but was introduced into Christian theology in the second century. What was it supposed to mean? The historical answer is: Not impassivity, unconcern, and impersonal detachment in the face of the creation. Not inability or unwillingness to empathize with human pain and grief, either. It means simply that God's experiences do not come upon him as ours come upon us. His are foreknown, willed, and chosen by himself, and are not involuntary surprises forced on him from outside, apart from his own decision, in the way that ours regularly are.[13]

By nature, God is both untethered to worldly concerns and intently caring at the same time. We as humans struggle with the exact opposite of this: at times we are too tethered to worldly concerns and lack an intent care for others. But as imperfect people, we experience these affections as a double-edged sword.

When the world around us causes a positive effect in our lives, such as through good friendship, then our virtue increases and we move a little bit more toward flourishing. But when the world around us causes a negative effect in our lives, such as through injustice, then our virtue decreases and we move a little bit away from flourishing. While our lives are more complicated than a mechanical process of one step forward, one step back, our lives are indeed a sea of affections buffeted by our beliefs and our actions in interaction with the world around us.[14] Not so God, who is wholly good and right, and so nothing that occurs here on Earth can change God's goodness and rightness.

One of the great things about being human is that we can grow. Christians believe that growth comes from being like Christ (see 1 Corinthians 11:1; Ephesians 4:22-24). This is a process that occurs over time and as the result of positive interactions with people and things around us: other believers, the Bible, the Holy Spirit, our pastor, and Christian radio, for example. But as technology advances, these interactions will change. The more that autonomous machines do everything for us, the more we are free to do what we want. Culture will whisper to us, "Sit in your Adirondack chair; you deserve it!" And we *will* sit in our Adirondack chairs, VR goggles strapped to our faces, autonomous lawnmowers whizzing around our yards. Increasingly we can become isolated from the world. Increasingly we become—and see ourselves—as impassible.

When it comes to our own lives, we get to choose our own world where we—not others, not God—get to define happiness for ourselves. No one can tell us to improve or get better when we have become impassible to the world around us. We don't put ourselves out there in ways that develop virtue. We lose opportunities to grow and minister to the world. We become little islands of discontentment—high on obligations but low on care for others.

This fits in well with parts of the transhumanist ideal. As Julian Huxley explains, "above all, that there are two complementary parts of our cosmic duty—one to ourselves, to be fulfilled in the realization and enjoyment of our capacities, the other to others, to be fulfilled in service to the community and in promoting the welfare of the generations to come and the advancement of our species as a whole."[15]

Notice what Huxley puts first—that our cosmic duty as people is "in the realization and enjoyment of our capacities." Nothing could be further from the truth. We are not gods, even if some among us think we are or can be. Our cosmic duty as people is to glorify God.

CLIMBING HIGH

One of the best stories of future-focused tech in the Bible is the story of the building of the tower of Babel (see Genesis 11:1-9). It's such a powerful story that it resonates with readers today on many levels. After the flood, the descendants of Noah worked together, speaking one language and sharing one culture. Over time, the nomadic tribes settled on the plains of Shinar. Using newly acquired tech, they became industrious, building with fire-formed bricks and tar mortar. With this they set out to make for themselves a great city—not only a great city, but a tower in the midst of the city that reached into the heavens. The people believed that this tower would make them famous and give them a symbol under which they could be united.

For the creators of the tower, the story doesn't end well. They put the tower up as a sign of their power for the world to see. But God wasn't thrilled with what they were doing and confused their languages so that they would not be united. As a result, the descendants of Noah now had different languages, and it caused them to separate and begin to scatter into other parts of the world. The building of the city and the tower came to an end.

In our time of modern tech, we know that we can't actually build a tower that will reach heaven. But we can build a society in which we have put ourselves at a distance from the rest of the world. If we let this occur, using autonomous machines and virtual reality to keep the world at a distance, we may fall into the age-old trap of being unaffected by the world.

Most people see the story of God's intervention in Babel in a negative way—that is, that God confused languages and brought division to people as a punishment, of sorts. But the truth may actually be the opposite of this. Maybe God, in his wisdom, did not want people to live above the rest of the world, cloistered away in a tower of their own making. Maybe God scattered the people not to punish them but to protect them from themselves.

We can't change the world if we are above it.

THREE
JURASSIC WORLD
GENE EDITING AND
BIOENHANCEMENT

You are acting like we are engaged in some kind of mad science.
But we are doing what we have done from the beginning.
Nothing in Jurassic World is natural. We have always filled gaps
in the genome with the DNA of other animals. And, if their
genetic code was pure, many of them would look quite different.
But you didn't ask for reality—you asked for more teeth.
—DR HENRY WU, *JURASSIC WORLD*

There may be twenty different types of dinosaurs in Jurassic World, but there's only one that people really talk about—the velociraptor. Created years before by InGen for the original Jurassic Park, the velociraptor is portrayed in the *Jurassic Park* movies as a pack animal that relies on pure instinct. It's a ferocious predator that until now seemed untamable by humans. When Masrani Global Corporation bought InGen, it opened a newly designed Jurassic World on Isla Nublar, an island off the coast of Costa Rica. Tourist revenue aside, Masrani Global also recommitted itself to the genetic engineering of dinosaurs and established strategic partnerships with worthwhile entities such as the U.S. military and the U.N. Security Council. In turn, Masrani Global appointed naval veteran Owen Grady to attempt to train velociraptors—a seemingly impossible task.

Hammond Creation Labs hatched four velociraptors for the experimental pack, and Grady tried two different but compatible methods to lead it: filial imprint and alpha male model.[1] In order to imprint himself on the velociraptors, Grady put himself in a maternal role once the velociraptors hatched. Just as a gosling follows its mother goose around without pause, a velociraptor hatchling would follow its "mother," Grady, in much the same way. After imprinting, Grady moved to the second method: asserting himself as the alpha of the pack, leading by feeding as well as other tried and true methods that work with many animals. Whether the training of this type of dinosaur species is even possible is a great unknown—clear results remain to be seen.

Actual velociraptors aren't anything like those depicted in the *Jurassic* movies, of course. Fossilized evidence shows that velociraptors were much smaller than humans and had feathers like birds; being chased by a real velociraptor would be like being chased by an angry turkey with a very long tail—a little dangerous, perhaps, but not too scary. The velociraptors in the movie more closely resemble what is known today as the Utahraptor, also part of the *Deinonychus* genus. Somehow "Utahraptor" just doesn't sound scary.

When the *Jurassic* movies create a fictional mashup of several different dinosaurs, we laugh and call it creative license. But what happens when gene editing technology allows us to create real-life mashups? Will we call it "creative license" when gene editing brings back a woolly mammoth by way of an Asian elephant hybrid?[2] Since they are close species, maybe. Will we call it "creative license" when gene editing merges sheep with humans? Probably not, especially since that moved from science fiction to science fact in 2018.[3]

Let's take it a few steps farther. What about when gene editing allows us to create a dog predator mashup for sport or military purposes? Actually, this is already on its way to science fact, as Chinese scientists created extra-muscular dogs way back in 2015.[4] And who wouldn't want a cute, cuddly, genetically modified micro-pig for their very own?[5] Or an endangered species paired with new defensive mechanisms mashup? And what about human mashups—the embryo of a human baby with Down syndrome paired with "healthy" human genes? And then there's the whole nothing-short-of-nutty "humanzee."[6]

To paraphrase a *Jurassic* sentiment: What could possibly go wrong?

SAMPLE TECH: GENE EDITING

Like virtual reality and autonomous machines, gene editing is a future technology that has already arrived in an initial stage today. Currently, the most common approach to gene editing is via CRISPR-Cas9. The main thing to know about this technology is that it has the power to cut out a gene that is unwanted—for example, a gene that makes a certain animal susceptible to a certain disease. It also has the power to insert a new gene in its place if needed—for example, if we want to add fluorescence to an animal's fur.[7] Illustrating the rapid ascent of technology is the fact that the CRISPR method went from idea to massive implementation for scientific study—more than 5,000 published papers—in only five years. And we can expect improvements to this method to continue rapidly.[8]

Scientists have already applied gene editing tech to crops, creating what are called genetically modified organisms (GMOs) or foods. This type of gene editing has met with fierce resistance in some parts of our world. Food scientists argue, however, that there is no scientific basis for avoiding most genetically modified foods.[9] Today, the debates are mostly about adding or subtracting a gene here or a gene there. Tomorrow, the debates will be about altering whole sections of genes, creating new hybrid plants and animals, and slates of alterations by which we can upgrade humans. The resistance to many of these ideas will only get fiercer.

Compared to gene editing, the challenges of virtual reality and autonomous machines seem rather small. We can take off the visor. We can choose not to buy every automaton on the market (perhaps I can refuse the Roomba lawnmower by telling myself I get exercise by cutting the grass by hand). But gene editing technology is quietly spreading around us—in our crops, in our livestock, in our medicines, and soon, in our bodies—faster than we can evaluate it and discern its proper role.

Speaking of spreading: if there ever was one genetic accident that has spread without ceasing, it is rats. Some readers may have a rat for a pet, but not me, sorry, never gonna happen (I'd rather have a pet snake). Rats are well-known carriers of disease and have a number of bad habits that humans find justifiably disgusting. They also can literally take over an island and destroy much of the native flora and fauna. That is what happened on Floreana, one of the Galapagos Islands, where introduced species of rats have wrought ecological havoc on the island for the past one hundred years. In a fascinating story in *WIRED*, Emma Harris reports on one possible solution ecologists are considering: using a special gene-editing technique called a *gene drive*, which would breed rats with a genetic predilection toward sterility in a lab and then release them into the rat population at large on Floreana.[10] If that happens, ecologists project it would eliminate all the rats on the small island in as few as five years. In other words, Floreana rat genocide.

If we have the tech to introduce a gene drive for sterility into rats by 2022, we could soon have a gene drive to introduce sterility into, well, whatever plant or bug or animal we don't like. I'm going to guess your next thought here. Yes, a mad scientist with minimal rogue government support could do this to people.

I can understand why God created rats. But I really do not understand why God created mosquitoes. I've been privy to one entomologist's defense of mosquitoes, but color me unconvinced.[11] I grew up in coastal Virginia, an area known for barrier islands that are completely infested with mosquitoes. Going to those islands gives new meaning to the expression "being eaten alive." Yet nothing in Virginia's islands ever made me fear the mosquito like spending time in rural Africa on mission trips. In many regions of Africa, the chance of catching malaria—a terrible disease that kills almost half a million people a year—is an ever-present danger.

Over a number of trips, I found it interesting to watch Westerners rationalize their approaches to a horrible disease that Africans face day in and day out. Some Westerners who traveled with me felt that God would help protect them from catching malaria—while they took precautions. Others thought that God would protect them from catching malaria, *without* precautions; still others took a laissez-faire malaria policy and simply didn't spend much time thinking about it. A few others were like me: utterly intent, every second of the day, not to let a mosquito near them. No matter what I was doing, in Africa I attuned my ears to the sound of that fateful buzz. I was determined to get every one of them before even one of them got me.

In the time that it took you to read the paragraph above, two more people died of malaria somewhere in the world. And two more will die before you reach the next page. Nearly a thousand before you reach the end of this book. Using soon-to-be-available technology such as a gene drive to eliminate malaria—even if it eradicates whole populations of certain mosquito species—seems to me the lesser evil.

From woolly mammoths to genocidal mosquitoes, tech such as gene editing seems a limitless Pandora's box that has arrived on our collective doorstep. What do we do with this box now that it has been opened? How far is too far? And who gets to decide?

PRAGMATISM 2.0

Gene editing illuminates the trend toward pragmatism within tech development. Pragmatism—the idea that if something "works," it must be "good"—started in North America in the late nineteenth century as a confluence of several philosophical ideas. It is perhaps not a true philosophy, in the sense of a system that explains the world; instead, pragmatism is more focused on helping make ideas work together.[12] Whereas some philosophies are largely unknown outside of college campuses (we're looking at you, Martin Heidegger), pragmatism has trickled into popular culture to such an extent that many people in the West view the world through a pragmatic lens. Coincidentally, pragmatism arose at the same time that technology had just started to take off on its seemingly exponential curve. From the sewing machine to the stapler, the world was undergoing rapid change.

As an idea system, pragmatism is quite appealing to tech enthusiasts, thinkers about the future, and transhumanists.[13] Since the advent of pragmatic thought, people increasingly believe that if a technology is effective in what it sets out to do, then it's ready for use. The focus was on the consequences of the idea and the action, not on long-term effects for society and people. When tech was only starting its rapid ascent, it was easy to foresee the consequences: a Pullman sleeping car brought luxury to journeying by train; a Gatling gun brought decisive victory to whoever put it to use. Yet the Gatling gun is an example of a new technology that had unforeseen consequences. Richard Gatling created his weapon with the idea that it might decrease casualties, but in the end, it only served to increase them (and start an arms race for automatic machine guns).[14]

As the tech curve swells, pragmatism—under the weight of tech innovation—is morphing into something new on the popular level. Contemporary pragmatic thinking goes like this: Can we build it? Then we should. Will it work? Let's try it and find out. This has become a mantra of our age. Governments, labs, and tech companies push forward with new tech under the argument that "if we don't do it, someone else will." This creates a whole new type of pragmatism that focuses less on consequences of actions and more on the power to act.

You may think *power* is not the right word there, but let's look at the questions again. Can we build it? Then we should.

This suggests that if we have the power to create, we must create. Will it work? Let's try it and find out. This suggests that if we believe we have the power to make something, we should make it—without thought to the consequences.

The new pragmatism is not well equipped to give us good solutions to the role of tech in the future. Saying we should create tech because we can is essentially the twenty-first-century version of "Might makes right." Many of us have seen enough remakes of King Arthur to know how flawed that argument is. Or as Jeff Goldblum's character in the original *Jurassic Park* famously quipped, "Your scientists were so preoccupied with whether or not they *could* that they didn't stop to think if they *should*."

Another flaw that comes by way of this new pragmatism for future tech is that it excuses naïveté. We invent tech or we use tech, and the consequences are not what we expect. We say to ourselves, "We didn't know that it would be used that way." As parents of young children, my wife and I hear variations of the same thing. "I gave my kindergartener an iPad, but I had no idea she would become addicted to it!" and "I gave my middle schooler a flux capacitor, but I had no idea he would attach it to a DeLorean and go back in time!" Over time, the buck gets passed from the tech creator to society to parents to kids. If you've been on this world for enough revolutions, you have seen this song and dance over and over again.

PREVENTION WITHOUT COMPROMISE

Gene editing is not an *if* nor a *when*. It is already beginning to occur. De-extinction is also a matter of when, not if. Call me Ben Franklin, but I fully expect to see a woolly mammoth (elephant hybrid) in my lifetime. The question that remains is what we edit, and how we go about it. Should we edit all species? Should we edit people? And to what degree? Should we edit out diseases? Should we edit out genetic chromosomal disorders like Down syndrome? Should we edit in improvements, such as perfect eyesight? Should we edit in designer upgrades, such as purple eye color or fluorescent skin? These are the questions that we should be asking before gene editing becomes the norm.

Even at this early stage, there are already serious questions. Let's look at Iceland. I love Iceland. It's a beautiful and unusual country, one that inhabits our imaginations more than our realities. I've only been there once—for a few days at the height of summer—and so I know there is a lot more to the place than what I've seen. Its otherworldly landscapes, lit up in July by an everlasting Arctic sun, show off hues that exist nowhere else on Earth. You never know whether you'll be able to wear shorts the next day or will be forced into a parka. You can walk on the edge of a glacier or overlook a fjord. It is but a glimpse of the wonders that God could do if pleasing people were God's primary task.

There's a darker side to Iceland, however, besides just their winter months. With the coming of genetic testing on infants in the past two decades, more and more Icelandic parents have chosen to abort fetuses at risk of Down syndrome. Even worse, since the test is only 85 percent accurate, an unknown number of non–Down syndrome babies have also been aborted out of caution—or fear. At this point, Iceland has almost "eradicated" Down syndrome.[15]

Yet when we talk of "eradicating" a genetic abnormality, what we can also mean is "eradicating" human lives. By any other name, this is eugenics. With the eradication of a few groups of people already occurring with basic genetic testing, what will happen once more advanced genetic editing arrives? And now that we have started eradicating people, where does it stop? People with Down syndrome? People with low IQs? People who are plump? People with red hair and green eyes?

One of the arguments marshaled in favor of improving humanity through the elimination of defective or inferior genetics is known as the *preventative principle*.[16] Simply put, this argument states that any disease or condition that we would be willing to treat or cure in adults we should be willing to treat or cure in babies in the womb. Thus, if we encounter an adult who has leukemia and we believe that is a disease worth treating (it is, of course), then we should also be willing to treat babies in the womb to prevent leukemia. Stated this way, the preventative principle does seem like a good starting point.

Yet this principle begins to fall apart once we get into specific situations. It makes assumptions about the nature of disease, and it sets up a half-truth about what it means to be a person. Let's look at specific examples.

We can all agree leukemia is a terrible disease and would stop at nothing to cure it. If we can cure it such that no child is born with leukemia in the future, even better. This is the preventative principle correctly applied. At this point in time, however, we can't cure leukemia in the womb. But through genetic testing, people can terminate pregnancies that evidence a high risk of leukemia, so that a child would not be born susceptible to leukemia.[17]

Earlier I said "stop at nothing," but would we really stop at nothing? Should someone terminate a pregnancy to prevent the spread of leukemia in their family? This harkens back to the basic puzzles we debated in college philosophy or ethics classes. The variation we encounter here is: "Would you let one person die if it meant sparing another from poor health?" To me, the answer is *no*. Yet for some people the answer would be *yes*. For many people, the end of apparently preventing (and therefore curing) leukemia in future generations would justify the means (or else they believe the baby in the womb is not a person yet).

Another problem with the preventative principle is that no two diseases are the same. We might "stop at nothing" (or almost nothing) to cure leukemia. Would we stop at nothing to cure near-sightedness? Like many readers, I suffer from this genetic defect. I can hardly see three feet in front of me without the assistance of technological innovation (eyeglasses). Yet some people who think it's ethical to terminate a pregnancy for leukemia risk would say it's unethical to terminate a pregnancy at risk for extreme nearsightedness. I'm not comparing leukemia to nearsightedness; I am simply pointing out that once we start down the slope of the preventative principle, it is a slippery one.

Genetic testing is only one stage of curing diseases through genetic therapy. The next stage is gene-editing babies in the womb. One day that technology will become highly successful. But no tech is perfect. Would we edit out leukemia from our unborn child if there is a 99 percent chance of success? I expect many people would say yes. How about 80 percent success? I expect we would start to lose many people at that point. Would we edit out nearsightedness if there was a 99 percent chance of success? For me, probably not; I would weigh a 1 percent loss of life as too great a risk for what I see as a "minor disease." But I am sure some would feel the risk was acceptable. Remember, in the future, if everyone has perfect vision, extreme nearsightedness would be considered a much more debilitating disorder than it is considered today.

Let me use a different example. Today, if I let my children grow up with teeth that look like they came from the seventeenth century—off-color, twisted, or crowded—people would think I was a negligent parent. Therefore, we spend what seems like a great deal of time at children's dentist and orthodontist offices. In the future, if a parent does not gene-edit their children for nearsightedness—even with a tiny risk of loss of life—they will likely be considered negligent parents. That kind of peer pressure will result in the adoption of both curative and enhancing tech. It is part of the addiction.

Moving further in this direction, one transhumanist suggests that since happiness is somewhat genetic, we could one day soon "cure" sadness by editing it out of our kids.[18] For those who thought I was reaching with the nearsighted example: let me assure you that this is a real proposal! Is sadness a disease? Of course, it can be. But would our world really be a better place if everyone were happy all the time? Would we take a tiny risk on the life of our child to "cure" them from sadness? What if that cure affected not only them but all their future descendants? What would happen if we lived in a world of perpetual happiness? It might be nice, but make no mistake: it wouldn't be heaven. Sin and injustice would still be a part of this world, making it seem fake to the point of being a mockery of God's plan.[19] We might be happier, but at the expense of being more blessed.

Let's hit the pause button. My head is spinning at this point, and maybe yours is, too. The possible outcomes and options are limitless, and the potential for problems is enormous. The preventative principle is less of a principle and more of a puzzle. Like any good puzzle, it is actually not very helpful when we apply it to real-world situations. Still, it seems likely that we will encounter it as tech picks up steam.

So when we hear someone argue that we should do *x* in order to prevent *y*, we need to make sure we read the fine print. The argument may not be as solid as it appears.

ADDITION WITHOUT REDUCTION

When I was a little kid, one of my favorite movies was Disney's *The Fox and the Hound*. Like many people, I rooted for Tod and imagined what it would be like to have a pet fox (I lived in rural Virginia, so it was possible, from a kid's perspective). Of course, foxes do not make good pets. Yet one of the most fascinating genetic experiments ever involved the creation of pet foxes.[20]

The Soviet Union of the mid-twentieth century boasted numerous fox farms that harvested fur for commercial purposes. These farms could be lucrative for the owners. The drawback is that foxes were not and could not be domesticated in the same way cows, horses, pigs, dogs, and cats are. Working with caged foxes was a risky business.[21] In the late 1950s, Dmitri Belyaev, a Russian geneticist, began an experiment to see if he could breed a friendly fox. The results were nothing less than startling. By only selecting the most "elite" foxes in terms of their acceptance of humans, he bred the foxes from wild and hostile to tame and docile in just forty generations. They are now so docile, in fact, that you can even buy one and keep it in your home. (At the time of this writing, $8,900 will get you a pet Russian silver fox that will follow you around and cuddle with you just like a dog).

But there's a wrinkle to this story. The original goal of the experiment was to breed tame foxes *in order to harvest their fur more quickly and easily*. Quicker and easier harvesting meant more money for the fox farm. As each successive generation of fox became tamer, they also started to look different. Gone was the prized black coat; it was replaced by patches of silver. Other physical changes—such as droopy ears, shorter tails, and changes in smell—also became a part of these foxes, as much as their tendency to be tame. While the domestication was a smashing success, the unintended consequences changed and even reduced these foxes into something a little less than fox-like.

The whole point of tech is to make our lives better. In some cases, though, technology can have a reductionist effect, which ends up making our lives a little less human (at least compared to past generations).

As I write this, the Alfie Evans case has recently rocked the United Kingdom and the world. Here was a child with a terminal illness; yet when the parents of the hospitalized child wished to seek alternative treatments or just continue treatments, the state prohibited the parents from choosing for their own child. This was even after the child was granted the opportunity for citizenship and travel to Italy. The High Court of Manchester rejected the parents' appeals, and the state terminated life support for Alfie, who passed away on April 28, 2018.[22] What should have been a joyous miracle—modern tech that might save a child's life—was usurped by an unbelievable callousness.

If we look back in history, we see that societies have always struggled to treat children well. Let's not forget what both Pharaoh and Herod did to children—and they were not even in the same culture and were separated in time by nearly 1,500 years. We live with a history of innumerable injustices toward children.

We also need to see the problem for what it really is: the injustice toward children stems not from tech but from the attitudes of people. What do Herod and the UK High Court of Manchester have in common? Not much, except that both assume the right to life and death over innocent children. I'm sure the High Court is just at times, as I am sure that Herod was just at times. Remember the old saying that even a broken clock is right two times a day.

The presumption of the High Court and Herod—that they are arbiters of justice for innocents—is unfounded. Shedding innocent blood is one of the things that the Lord hates (Proverbs 6:16-17). This presumption also reveals a severe flaw in humanity: we think that we are in charge. Our decision is what stands. Technology is just the latest tool to confirm our mistaken impression that we have authority over our universe. What authority we possess, though, is self-appointed, and it is nothing compared to the authority of our Creator.

SOVEREIGNTY

Everyone wants to believe they have the right to do what they want to do. If I want to buy and use a karaoke machine, I have the right to do so (consider yourself forewarned). If I want to live in a house painted green, I have the right to do so (and hopefully there is no homeowners association). If I want to fight for the life of my child against seemingly impossible odds, I have the right to do so. If I want to end the life of an unborn baby over whom I have legal authority, I have the right to do so.

All this stems from the myth we come to accept at an early age: This is my life, and I am seated on the throne of it. No matter what befalls me, I reign over myself. Like most lies in our world, this is a half-truth. This life *is* my life. But because I have rebelled against my Creator, if I want to have real life, I need to step out of trying to control my life, and allow God to rule in my life. As Creator, God is sovereign over our world, and everything in it, including me. We are not actually in charge, even if we think that we are.

God's sovereign nature is rooted in ideas of divine king-ship that permeated the ancient world. Most people in the Western world know the opening part of Psalm 23: "The Lord is my shepherd; I shall not want (ESV)." People hear this in church and at funerals. They find comfort in hearing about green pastures and still waters. In our culture, the image of a shepherd makes them think of a kindly old man who is tender and gentle.

This image is not totally wrong, but it's not entirely accu-rate either. In the ancient world, shepherds were not tender; they were men of strength who were in charge of large herds of animals. They were armed and fought off wild animals like lions and bears as well as human attackers. David was a shepherd, and alongside his anointing and valiance, he was also strong enough as a young man to kill Goliath and cut off his head (see 1 Samuel 16–17). Furthermore, in Ancient Near Eastern cultures, a shepherd was a symbol for a strong king. Just as a shepherd ruled over and protected his flocks, so a king ruled over and protected his people.

In that sense, Psalm 23 is less a reminder of God's tender-ness than a declaration of God's sovereignty. Since the Lord is my King, I will not have needs. I can have an abundant life because God is strong and mighty, guiding me and protecting me.

In Jesus, the sovereignty of God is most made known in our world. As the Puritan pastor and theologian Jonathan Edwards explains, "Christ is the Creator, and great possessor of heaven and earth: he is sovereign Lord of all: he rules over the whole universe, and doth whatsoever pleaseth him: his knowledge is without bound: his wisdom is perfect, and what none can circumvent: his power is infinite, and none can resist him: his riches are immense and inexhaustible: his majesty is infinitely awful."[23]

The shepherd of green pastures and still waters is the same God who is ruler of the universe, infinitely awe-ful. In Christian belief, God is seated on the throne and Jesus is at God's right hand (see Ephesians 1:20). In modern practice, the individual is seated on the throne and technology is at the person's right hand. Instead of God-focused ideas like those of Edwards, transhumanism points to human-focused ideas like that of Renaissance philosopher Giovanni Pico della Mirandola in *Oration on the Dignity of Man*:

> We have made you a creature neither of heaven nor of earth, neither mortal nor immortal, in order that you may, as the free and proud shaper of your own being, fashion yourself in the form you may prefer. It will be in your power to descend to the lower, brutish forms of life; you will be able, through your own decision, to rise again to the superior orders whose life is divine.[24]

Laying aside Mirandola's rhetorical power—it is a stirring sentiment—these ideas only serve to obscure the weaknesses innate in our own human nature. We can shape ourselves, but we cannot shape ourselves *well*. We are not rulers of our own world; we are not self-reliant, nor are we unaffected by the world. We are mortal, and without God's help, we remain only in the lower, brutish form of life.

Most future tech will prove wonderful for our time here on Earth. But when culture tries to tell us that by this tech we can rule our world, don't believe it. Tech can never legitimately put us on the throne.

ANOINTED WITH OIL

Perhaps the most well-known of Jesus' parables is the parable of the good Samaritan. Western culture promotes this story in part because it fits well into the humanist narrative—that people are the great saviors of our world. As such, the Samaritan can be cast as the ideal humanist.

This is not Jesus' point, of course; his point was that followers of God are called to love their neighbors regardless of tribe or circumstance (see Luke 10:36). One way to do this is to show mercy for those in need (see Luke 10:37). Though it is not the primary point of the story, we do see technology in action in Jesus' parable.

One way the Samaritan shows love to his neighbor is by treating the man's wounds. Notice that when the Samaritan discovers the man, he doesn't simply pray for the man; he applies medical assistance through technology. We notice that the Samaritan uses three types of tech: bandages, wine, and oil. Each one is a form of tech that the Samaritan would have had to purchase (or make) in advance.

In this parable, Jesus uses three different medical technologies to show to his audience the great care that the Samaritan applies to the wounded man. As modern readers, we understand the use of two of these: wine (for cleaning) and bandages (for binding). The use of oil is a bit less clear. In the Old Testament, oil almost always refers to either the commodity itself or its cosmetic applications (including anointing). Only in the New Testament do we really encounter oil used in an overtly medicinal manner.[25]

This has led to confusion in other passages of Scripture, notably in the passage in which James asks, "Is anyone among you sick?" and then suggests, "Let him call for the elders of the church, and let them pray over him, anointing him with oil in the name of the Lord" (James 5:14 ESV). In this case, the oil is used by the elders as a natural part of the healing process. Much like soap for early Americans, oil was used by Ancient Near Eastern peoples for medicinal purposes, even though its actual role in the healing process was not well understood. But early Christians understood that using oil and other physical curatives complemented the power of prayer. God's direct or indirect action is what ultimately heals, but tech creates greater opportunities for healing to occur.

From oil to soap to antibiotics to gene therapy, tech increasingly gives humanity greater ability to treat physical ailments. And I say, "Praise God for that" and give thanks for and to all the men and women who work in medicine, past and present, to make our lives better.

But treating physical illness is only part of the redemption of humanity. Whether it be the miracles God does to heal some or the possibility of salvation for all, redemption is from God and God alone. People may be able to help each other, but only God can rescue us from our human condition. God is the strong shepherd who leads us to better places and restores our bodies, minds, and souls.

FOUR

PASSENGERS

ARTIFICIAL INTELLIGENCE AND THE MASTERS OF THE UNIVERSE

Jim: *Let's say you figured out how to do something that would make your life a million times better, but you knew it was wrong, and there's no taking it back.... how do you do the math?*

Arthur: *Jim, these are not robot questions....*

Jim: *What am I going to do?*

Arthur: *I'm here for you.*

Jim: *Arthur, you're a machine. [Jim pokes Arthur]. See? See? See, you can't feel that, you don't have feelings! See, that doesn't hurt, and you don't even mind—because you're not a person.*

—PASSENGERS

Arthur loved his life. Truth be told, his life centered around his job—serving as the bartender aboard the starship *Avalon*. Nothing pleased Arthur more than taking care of the ship's guests. They would wander in and, in what seemed like a nanosecond, share a wide assortment of personal details about their thoughts, their feelings, and their lives. Some nights it wasn't too busy, and on those nights Arthur could really pay attention to his guests. Of course, Arthur had learned long ago not to hover around his patrons; that made them nervous. Instead, Arthur busied himself polishing glasses so that it looked as if he were busy—a trick of the trade—when in fact he was hanging on their every word. Admittedly, Arthur's work didn't allow much time to entertain certain types of pleasurable pursuits, such as reading. But then again, androids don't read.

Arthur is indicative of the way we expect androids—robots that look like humans with artificial intelligence (AI)—to act. Even though we have never met an android, we expect them to be precise, accurate, and above all else, knowledgeable. That knowledge, coupled with the ability to speak and interact, may tempt people to believe that their interactions with forms of artificial intelligence will, over time, become more than the sum of the AI's programming. In the movie *Passengers*, Jim finds out that this is never the case. Arthur's programming is limited to his programming. There is nothing more there. There is no relationship—only communication based on algorithms.

Arthur of the starship *Avalon* is typical of one type of robot we meet in movies about the future. In essence, Arthur is a robot that can do a few simple tasks and has the ability to verbally exchange information with people. His programming is based on a moderately sophisticated AI that covers areas such as ship information and human conversation dynamics.

I say *moderately* sophisticated because some of the questions Jim asks Arthur about the ship could be answered by something not much more powerful than Amazon's Alexa or Apple's Siri. And much of the rest—knowing how to respond to general human communication ("chit chat")—is actually not much of a leap away in terms of our technology today. In several cases, Jim asks a question that is outside of Arthur's AI range, which prompts Arthur to respond with a standardized expression meant to not answer Jim but make Jim *feel* like he is being answered.[1] Putting all this together in a mechanical form that can do small, repetitive tasks is the only thing holding us back from having our own Arthur in a matter of years.

Arthur's creators intended his smile and soothing voice to put humans at ease. And who is threatened by a mild-mannered bartender?

Not all AI, though, will be like Arthur. What happens when we encounter AI that is not "obvious" like Arthur? What happens when we find out AI is working behind the scenes to make decisions for us, especially in ways that we cannot see or understand? How do we adapt to the coming AI revolution, when much of what will occur will not be easily visible on the smiling face of a friendly android?

SAMPLE TECH: ARTIFICIAL INTELLIGENCE

There is one thing that virtual reality, autonomous machines, gene editing, and artificial intelligence have in common: All four are science fact, not science fiction. Artificial intelligence is here, and it is already all around us.

"Wait, wait!" I can hear some people respond. "There are no computers or robots that talk to us without being programmed. How can you say that artificial intelligence is already here?"

To answer this, we need to delve into what *artificial intelligence* means. Among technology experts, there are many different definitions for AI, which can make it hard to pin down a simple answer. When many of us think of AI, we think of the computers that talk to people in sci-fi movies. Let's be honest: that is a very compelling view of AI. It is basically AI set in a real-world application. Yet actual AI proves to be much more basic—and in the long run, much more powerful—than the rather obvious AI of sci-fi movies. To grasp AI, we need to grasp algorithms.

When I interview students for our graduate ministry program, one of the standard questions we ask is "What was your least favorite subject in high school and college?" I can't prove it, but it seems like 99.994 percent of all incoming students answer, "Math." Yes, math stinks.

I'm kidding; math is actually pretty awesome. When I was growing up, I didn't always do well in my math classes. But then I went to a regional math contest for high school students, and—I know I'm losing cool points here—I came in second place. This came as a shock to me and even more of a shock to my math teacher.

As I discovered later in life, one of the problems I had with math as a subject is that I never understood how it related to the real world. It was just *so* boring! In college, I took years of calculus, elementary differential equations, and more. But I still never did well in any of those classes because I never understood why any of it mattered. Only later in life did I began to realize how important math is, and I learned that only because I learned about real-world applications. I believe this is one of the major reasons why people unfairly hate math.

At its most basic, artificial intelligence is nothing more than a complex math formula called an algorithm. An algorithm is a set of instructions that can be used to guide a person or machine to a conclusion. An algorithm is designed to use a lot of data to solve a boring problem to get an important answer.

When we combine multiple algorithms, we get a scenario that we today call artificial intelligence.

Go with small children to almost any sit-down restaurant in North America today and you will receive colorful kids' menus and crayons. Often on those menus you'll see something that looks like a large hashtag—a tic-tac-toe playing grid. When my family and I go out to eat at these kinds of restaurants, my kids enjoy challenging me to tic-tac-toe games. When they were very young, we'd play and I'd always win. When they were a little older (but still young enough to be interested), we would play and I would always win or it would be a draw.

Reading this, you may wonder if I am the world's greatest tic-tac-toe player. Sorry, but no; tic-tac-toe is a simple game that has simple rules that determine whether a person will win, lose, or draw. If you master these simple instructions, you will always win or draw. Because my children did not understand the rules well, they did not win.

These rules of tic-tac-toe are essentially algorithms that I have learned and mastered, even if I never called them that or understood them in that way. My mind then combines these rules into a workable whole that gives me "tic-tac-toe intelligence."

It is no wonder, then, that AI makes headlines when it comes to games such as tic-tac-toe, chess, or Go. Humans can program algorithms to account for instructions in those games, and the computer can assemble those instructions in order to create "chess intelligence" or some other form. The important thing to remember at this point is that there is a big difference between my tic-tac-toe intelligence and a computer's chess intelligence. My intelligence lets me make illogical moves, and it allows me to switch to doing a word search once my child bores of tic-tac-toe, whereas the computer's intelligence does not. At least not yet.

AIs that play chess have evolved past this simplistic explanation. The latest and greatest chess AI is Google's AlphaZero, which taught itself chess in just four hours—and then went on to beat the previous world's best chess program.[2] Yet these AIs are still very much of a type of AI referred to as *narrow AI*. Narrow AI is a type of machine intelligence that can think through one type of thing—like chess or tic-tac-toe—really well but cannot think about other types of things—like word searches or what little kids want to eat—at all.[3]

Increasingly we are in a world surrounded by algorithms and narrow AI. When we upload a photo of our friends and Facebook suggests the names of each of those people, that is a narrow AI, powered by sophisticated algorithms that determine who to tag. Likewise, facial recognition technology also works off cameras attached to an AI.[4] In the near future, when you go to a doctor for a checkup, an AI will analyze your health. And when you go to a bank, an AI will analyze your financial health.

Narrow AI works well when it comes to probability and predictability. For example, by using algorithms and crunching large amounts of data, Google has created a way to predict heart disease simply by looking at pictures of your eyes.[5] And researchers at Purdue University have unveiled a new AI called Chat Analysis Triage Tool (CATT), which can identify adults who are attempting to lure children into offline sexual scenarios.[6] In the near future, these kinds of AIs will power devices in our homes. The future versions of Alexa and Siri will be great at answering questions such as "What should I have for supper tonight?" and "What do most Americans like to do on vacation?" In fact, the sheer number of narrow AIs that people will possess and interact with seems limitless at this point.

What happens when someone takes a bunch of narrow AIs and gets them to work together? What happens when a computer can play chess *and* tic-tac-toe? Add to that the recent situations in which a computer can solve a Rubik's cube and another AI can win against a human in a structured debate scenario. Add similar advances that are coming seemingly every month now.[7]

That's where we edge closer to general AI. This is a type of artificial intelligence that can do many different kinds of things well. Sometimes people liken general AI to "thinking like a human being," but theorists debate what that really looks like. Some theorists argue that algorithms will simply become more and more complex until there is a "master algorithm" that controls all of these narrow AIs.[8] This would be a miraculous technology, "smarter" than humans in most ways but still lacking what we would call self-awareness. By this definition, this type of AI is still less intelligent than a common housecat. But it would be able to do more than tell us what we should have for dinner. It would be able to answer questions that we can't answer and, perhaps, questions we don't even know to ask.

Closing in on general AI will make this tech seem alien, maybe even godlike, to the casual observer. We will need to buckle up if we are going to brave this future well.

OUR FLATTENED WORLD

Growing up with parents who worked for NASA, I was bound to be interested in the sciences, especially astronomy. Also, growing up in rural Virginia meant when I went outside on a warm summer night, I could really see the stars in the sky (until the mosquitoes forced me back inside). I still remember looking at the stars and thinking about God "up there." That's the third piece of this story: being raised in the Western philosophical tradition, I believed God to be out in space somewhere. Not that I was aware of it at the time, but that's how I saw the universe. I didn't understand that creation was, for all purposes, boundless, and that God stood outside of a vast universe that he had created. And as a human, I stood on the earth, above the animals and the plants, who couldn't look at the stars like I could.

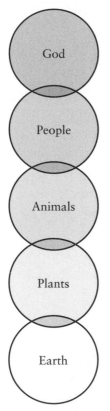

This view of the world made sense to me—God, people, the rest of creation.

Though this basic idea about our world has stood for several millennia, our world is changing. Western philosophical tradition has been criticized for years, to the point where its time in the sun is likely coming to an end. I'm not going to defend this tradition. While it is not wholly incompatible with Christian thought, it is also not a biblical worldview. Yet some of the philosophies vying to replace the Western tradition will prove to be worse in the long run for several reasons.

First, the idea of God has begun to shrink. Is there a God? Probably not, the thinking goes. And since humanity has slowly but surely evolved to the pinnacle of known existence, we can ourselves become gods. Second, the place of animals and plants has increased in this newer worldview. Humans are, after all, animals, genetically very similar to monkeys, pigs, squirrels, and most everything else than inhabits our planet. Plants are part and parcel of our world also.

In sum, what is occurring is a flattening of the way we look at our world. In the twenty-first century, the prevailing worldview could, ironically, be thought of as almost a "flattened earth" perspective: that is, a perspective in which God is absent and humans are merely animals.

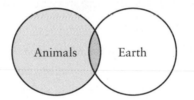

In this scenario, there are only organics and inorganics, the living and the nonliving. Everything that is organic is united by the same biology, the same genetics, the same rights, the same purposes. Humans have no more right to evolve than apes or sloths. There is no God or gods or heavenly beings; there is only matter. Humans, who are animals, do not have the right to shape other animals, but we do have the right to shape matter. Using energy, we can turn matter into anything we want: buildings, robots, Martian rovers, or light sabers.

You may have expected tech to be in one of the circles, given the worldview I'm describing. It's not, because in this perspective tech is viewed as a force (tool), not an entity (agent). With tech, animals (people) will shape earth (matter) and other animals (people, animals, and plants). If this worldview fully comes to pass, there will be several major implications for using technology:

- There is nothing above us (no God) to whom we are accountable.
- There is nothing below us to which we are responsible; everything is mutable.
- As a result, tech acquires an increasingly disproportionate influence in our world.
- The greater the influence of tech, the faster our world will seem flattened.
- The more flattened the world becomes, the lower humanity goes and the greater the possibility that tech will supplant us.

This shifting landscape says a great deal more about culture than it does about tech. But tech is highly influenced by culture and comes to us through culture—via marketing and distribution. As future tech arrives, it will encourage humanity to see itself in a different light than it did several hundred years ago. In this, humanity will not have evolved in the true sense of the word. Instead, only our understanding of science will have improved. But from the perspective of previous generations of humanity, and to people at that time, they will believe they have evolved. The true posthumans—meaning humans after a tech singularity (explained below)—will think of themselves as almost godlike, not above their world in the classical tradition but united and attuned to everything in it. If this occurs, the true posthumans will suffer delusions of grandeur that their ancestors could only dream of.

THE SINGULARITY

Speaking of delusions of grandeur: one of the great dreams of our world today is the singularity. What could cause us to evolve into a posthuman future? The singularity could. If it even exists.[9]

The *singularity* refers to a possible event in the near future in which the power of technology approaches the infinite. There are various explanations for how the singularity will occur. One of the most popular is that we will invent a general AI that is as smart as a person, with all the data of our world at its disposal. When I say "all the data of our world," I don't mean merely data we have collected to that point. Instead, that AI will likely be connected to the Internet of Things (IoT), a near-future scenario in which not just computers but your home appliances and cars are attached to the internet and sending and receiving data. This creates a never-ending stream of new data—a stream that a general AI could access.

As soon as we create a general AI that is as smart as a human being, it is only a small step until that general AI becomes smarter than a human, and then on its own becomes smarter and smarter and smarter still, at a never-ending pace. Just like the chess AIs. The worry, of course, is that whereas a narrow AI can checkmate a human player in the game of chess, a general AI could checkmate human civilization in the game of life. In other words, the robots-take-over-the-world scenario of the *Terminator* movies becomes imaginable. Killer robots aside, if a singularity does occur, it would be the end of the world as we know it (emphasis on the "as we know it" part, as the new world could turn out to be a more pleasant place to live, at least compared to the hard lives of previous generations).[10]

The best way to envision the singularity is along a curve on a graph, which starts out slowly moving to the right and upward. As it moves horizontally, its upward movement

increases more and more until it turns almost completely vertical. It's like when I was in middle school: I kept measuring
myself and hoping I would get taller. It seemed like a quarter
of an inch here and there—until one day it seemed I grew a
foot and the next thing I knew, I was at my adult height. That
is the way the singularity will happen—again, if it happens
at all.

The singularity has its own evangelists—tech prognostica-
tors like Vernor Vinge and Ray Kurzweil—and its own evidence that demands a verdict, like Moore's law (the rule that
essentially says computing power will double every eighteen
months). There are plenty of detractors as well, thinkers who
believe tech gains are irregular or come in waves, or who argue
we are one disaster away from rendering our world unfixable.
Still, the idea that technology is going to take off even more
than it has now, and revolutionize the world we live in, fits in
well with the transhumanist narrative. We can save humanity
if we just make it to the next big abacus, cotton gin, internet,
or medical tricorder.

A great deal of ink has already been spilt trying to describe
the singularity, yet it is something that cannot be described. If
it occurs, the change in human society will be so great that the
before and after will look nothing alike. However, most of the
people talking about the singularity are talking about it from
a societal perspective, not a personal perspective. The singularity may solve world hunger, but it won't make you happy
(unless you edit out your sad genes). This is where most of the
descriptions of the singularity fall short. Everything changes,
except human nature.

So is there a singularity coming? If you make me answer, I
will say *yes*—with one big caveat. That caveat is that we really

don't know where on the curve we are at present, nor exactly what the upward axis represents. To put it more simply, I do believe that technology is increasing at a rate that will never decrease, short of some type of world-ending, apocalyptic scenario. However, we simply do not know what that rate actually means.

To use my earlier height example, let's say that in middle school I was the only person on Earth. (That sure would have made middle school a lot easier.) Even though I was alone, I kept measuring myself, hoping to get taller. I thought I would get taller, and some signs I could see around me suggested I would get taller. But being the only person on Earth, I had no way to know for sure. I also had little idea how tall I would get, or how long it would take to achieve optimum height, because I was the only one on Earth. It *seemed* like I was growing, but there was nothing I could compare it to, nor any way to find out what my height really meant. (Was I still short, or was I inordinately tall?)

Yes, there is a singularity coming, but when it will happen and what it actually means—well, we have no idea. The upside, if I'm wrong and the singularity never happens? It will be much easier to brave the future.

While it's pretty difficult to say much about the coming singularity, it's pretty easy to guess how culture will use any big bang of tech growth. In fact, we've seen it before. During the run-up to the Industrial Revolution, people predicted the rapid increase in tech would signal the end of religion. God is dead, and all that.[11] This is the prevailing trend toward a flattened world, as I noted above. The greater humans are, the less we need God—or at least, that is what culture tries to tell us.

The good news is that it doesn't seem to be working as well as culture hoped. Let's assume for a moment that the Industrial Revolution marks the beginning of the first noticeable tick upward on the singularity graph. It's like the first half-inch I noticed I grew back in middle school—it opened my eyes to the possibility I really was going to get taller. As the Industrial Revolution evolved into the Space Age, society as a whole tried to distance itself from religion, but your average person didn't necessarily get less religious.

Some may ask, "But what about Western Europe? It's almost totally secular." I would counter with, "What about China, Rwanda, and Brazil? The church is spreading like wildfire." In other words, the gospel's influence has moved, but it has not been quenched. In fact, technology has no impact on what God will and will not do in our world.

When it comes to this subject, my favorite color is jade. No matter what tech advances occur while I am alive, I know some cultural media barometer will declare it to have a devastating effect on the Christian faith.[12] Don't believe it. From the construction of Stonehenge to the astrolabe, the discovery of longitude, the phlogiston theory, the theory of evolution, holodecks, phasers set on stun, and the discovery of life on other worlds, none of these things casts any doubt on who God is. All those examples, and any more that you could come up with, exist in the physical universe defined by space and time. God is outside of space and time, so whatever occurs in space and time is irrelevant to God's nature and plans. God is a lot bigger than predicted by cultural media barometers.

There's a second part to this. Remember the flattened world above? The thing about removing God from our worldview means that other things have to take the place of what we perceive as God. Transhumanists—and many others who have never even heard of that term—hope the basis for that is a utopia that comes through technology. But in this scenario, there is nothing "above" us and nothing "below" us; there are just animals and earth, organics and inorganics. So the push will be to love your fellow organics.[13]

There are, in a sense, two great laws of our universe: love God and love the people around you as if they were your own. When the expert in the law asked Jesus about the greatest commandment, Jesus quoted from Deuteronomy and Leviticus: "'Love the Lord your God with all your heart and with all your soul and with all your mind.' This is the first and greatest commandment. And the second is like it: 'Love your neighbor as yourself'" (Matthew 22:37-39). Those of us who follow Jesus know these commandments lead to wholeness and truth and abundant life.

It's often said that half a truth is half a lie—honoring one law and denying the other is living a lie. We will never be blessed if we try to honor the creation without honoring the Creator (or vice versa, for that matter). Either version is a Jesus-less gospel; it has never worked, it doesn't work now, and it never will.

But that won't stop culture from trying, yet again, to see if this time honoring the creation without honoring the Creator will stick. In a flattened world, a horizontal reach is the only play you have.

MASTERS OF THE UNIVERSE

Of all the future tech we'll cover in this book, artificial intelligence gets the most press. It's a hot topic, in part because it is the easiest one to link to some kind of end-of-the-world scenario. Nothing generates hits, clicks, and page views like the apocalypse.

It is true that humans increasingly perceive tech to be the most powerful force in the universe. Having said that, I stand by my original statement: tech is merely a tool that is given its force, power, and influence by people. As narrow AI edges closer to general AI and infiltrates every aspect of our existence, we may begin to feel powerless against it. Years ago, if I went through security at an airport and was subjected to a metal detector or the wand, I may have felt annoyed. Now, when I go through the naked body scanner, I feel powerless. AI is to the computer what the naked body scanner is to the metal detector. This powerlessness is symptomatic of a larger issue.

In the history of the human race, humans have recognized four different "masters of the universe"—that is, sources of authority. These masters do not necessarily represent any one specific individual, but they are paradigms for understanding the way people perceive power in relation to their own lives. Three are in the past or present, and one is still in the future. These four masters of the universe are gods, kings, hearts, and tech. Let's consider the reign of each.

In the ancient world, gods were the masters of the universe. People believed in the gods and thought that pleasing the gods was critical for human flourishing. Rejecting the gods was something you just didn't do (we're looking at you, Socrates). To obey the gods meant being obedient to the universal order. There was nothing greater than the gods, and they spoke with authority over all and had power over all. Their power seemed limitless compared to humanity's power. It was impossible to know much about the gods; they were unfathomable. The way to influence the gods was through sacrifice. But in the end, the

GODS	Obedience: Universal Order Power: All powerful Knowing: Unfathomable Influence: Sacrifice Result: Capricious
KINGS	Obedience: Local Order Power: Very powerful Knowing: Possibly fathomable Influence: Fealty Result: Capricious
HEARTS	Obedience: Individual Order Power: Personally powerful Knowing: Very fathomable Influence: Romance Result: Capricious
TECH	Obedience: Collective Order? Power: Impersonally powerful? Knowing: Too fathomable? Influence: Use? Result: Capricious

feeling most people had was that the gods were capricious and inconsistent in their dealings with humans.

In the medieval world, kings were the masters of the universe. This doesn't mean that gods ceased to exist, it just means that human leadership moved into a primary role. Being obedient to a king meant fitting within the local order. Kings were very powerful, but their power was not limitless. While the thoughts of kings were above the thoughts of peasants, they were still human and it was possible, at least in some cases, to grasp their ways. The way kings expected to be pleased was through fealty; you could influence kings through your loyalty to them. But in the end, the feeling most people had was that kings, like the gods, were capricious.

In the modern world, human individuals (hearts) are the masters of the universe. This doesn't mean gods and kings aren't around anymore as sources of authority; it just means that the thoughts, feelings, and rights of individuals moved into a primary role. Being obedient to one's own heart meant fitting into a local order. That local order could be a nation, a state, a county, a village, a family, or just you yourself—really, whatever your heart tells you would probably be fine. Hearts are very powerful, but their power has a very limited range—sometimes less than a few people. Hearts are meant to be known, and their thoughts are very accessible in most situations. The way the heart wants to be pleased is romance; not "romance" in the sense of country music ballads or rom-coms, but in the sense of focus on emotion, subjectivity, and individuality.[14] But, in the end, the feeling most people have is that individuals, too, are capricious.

It's easy to summarize the past. But what about the future? What will be the master of universe in the future? And what kind of master will it be?

In the future world, tech will be the master of the universe. This doesn't mean that gods, kings, and hearts won't be around; it just means that the tech will fully encroach on every area of our lives and will move into a primary role. Being obedient to tech will probably mean fitting into a collective order based on tech development. Tech is very powerful, but since it is a tool that often hides the intent of its user, it will likely be deeply impersonal (and painfully so). Tech will be known, but it will likely change the way we learn about and know ourselves and each other—it will likely lay bare many of the remaining mysteries of the world.[15] Future tech will only be pleased when we use it, which will be all the time. But in the end, the feeling most people will have is that tech is capricious.

Meet the new master of the universe—same as the old master of the universe. But these paradigms for understanding the way people perceive power in relation to their own lives omits one factor: a God who is wholly above human power. Gods, kings, hearts, and tech all have transactional relationships with people. The God of the Bible does not.

OMNISCIENCE

When I was in graduate school in North Carolina, I volunteered to go to New Hampshire as part of a small mission team. Our team rented a van and headed north through seven states. During my turn driving, the team member riding in the passenger seat peppered me with questions about theology. Several hours later, after pontificating on the mysteries of God, it dawned on me that I had driven us through two wrong states. We had to turn around and backtrack (though it gave me even more time for further pontification). Even today, sometimes my wife will not let me "talk and drive."

If I were honest for a moment, I would admit I'm sensitive about being an "absent-minded professor." The stereotype hits a little too close to home. I definitely struggle at times with what people affectionately call "common sense." When you can't find your keys or cell phone, you might call it a "bad day." I call that "every day." I get preoccupied with my thoughts rather easily.

By universal standards, my thoughts are not that deep. I am a human, which means my knowledge or intellect is no more than a tapeworm or a spinach leaf next to God's. My thoughts are nothing compared to God's thoughts, and my ways are incomparable to God's ways. No animal can think as God thinks. Because I trust in God, I can admit that without hesitation.

Humanity believes that we as a species are knowledgeable, but in fact this is not true at all. Our vaunted intelligence is minimal compared to any universal measurement. The only thing we can know as people is within our sphere of detection: what we can see and touch and taste and smell and hear, and whatever we reason from these detections. But since we are extremely limited in time and space, we can detect very little, which means we can reason very little as well. True, what we have been able to reason is quite significant to us, quite impressive by any yardstick of our own. But God's knowledge of our world is vastly different from ours.

This is why we describe God as *omniscient*. While it is true that the word means "all-knowing," the term *omniscient* has many more implications that just unlimited knowledge. For example, Dutch theologian Herman Bavinck explains, "God knows things not by observation, but from and of himself. Our knowledge is posterior: it presupposes their existence and is derived from it. Exactly the opposite is true of God's knowledge: he knows everything before it exists. Scripture expresses this very clearly when it states that God knows all that happens before it happens (Isa. 46:10; Amos 3:7; Dan. 2:22; Ps. 139:6; Matt. 6:8; etc.)."[16]

In other words, our knowledge is forever limited because it is based on only what we can see, looking back, from our own very, very limited perspective. But God bases knowledge on an eternal and universal perspective outside of creation.

To put it another way, we are like fish in a fishbowl. We can only observe our immediate surroundings. Through reason, we could possibly one day figure out that we are in a bowl and perhaps make things better in the bowl. But we can never get outside of the bowl. God is outside the bowl, but also gets in the bowl from time to time just because God loves us. The most meaningful example of this is the incarnation.

Because God is omniscient and we are not, it is quite possible for our knowledge on an issue to be so limited, so feeble, so impoverished that we really don't understand the issue at all—even when we are convinced we know quite a bit. Proof of this is easily demonstrable in the scientific theories that were created, promoted, believed, disproved, and eventually discarded: from the phlogiston theory to the aether idea to the use of strychnine to treat cholera. To be fair, trying new things is the way science works; it is a good thing to discover the way God made the world. To say it better: trying new things is good as long as we understand our role and our limitations. When culture encourages us to believe that humanity's knowledge is *not* limited, hubris will grow like weeds in the hearts of people. Hubris and tech should never be mixed.

TOOLS OF DIVINATION

Today when we think of sciences, we think of disciplines such as physics, chemistry, math, and engineering. These were sciences in the ancient world (to whatever lesser degree they were understood), but there were also other "sciences." One was divination. Divination is not exactly the same as magic, which is an attempt by people to get spiritual entities to act on their behalf; instead, divination is an attempt to discover the future or the unknown by tapping into the spiritual realm. The "science" of divination even came with its own technologies, examples of which are noted in the Bible: "For the king of Babylon will stop at the fork in the road, at the junction of the two roads, to seek an omen: He will cast lots with arrows, he will consult his idols, he will examine the liver" (Ezekiel 21:21).

Since we don't often hear people talking about Ezekiel 21, here is a bit of background: This part of Ezekiel is a proclamation by God through Ezekiel of the coming destruction of Jerusalem by the Babylonians. Ezekiel is creating a picture of how this judgment will come about, even though the people of Jerusalem are not listening. Part of this picture is that the king of Babylon will use the technologies of divination to create a plan to lay siege to Jerusalem. The Babylonian king doesn't rely on just one tech; he uses three different ones. First, he shoots or shakes arrows to discover how they will land (belomancy); second, he attempts to receive a dream or vision from an idol (teraphim); and third, he examines the liver of an animal sacrificed to the gods (hepatoscopy).[17] Ezekiel is likely making this point: the king will stop at nothing to determine the most auspicious approach to attack Jerusalem.

From a modern perspective that struggles to accept the spiritual world, divination and AI would seem to have nothing in common. But if we look at these two sciences from an anthropological perspective, there are actually quite a number of striking parallels.

Divination was the science of learning the unknown. Diviners used tech in an attempt to discover the unknown so that it made sense to them based on their understanding of the world. No one today would examine a liver to try to learn something about the universe. But that's only because the science on which the idea is based has become outdated. The diviner was someone who tried to know more about the universe than they could themselves detect or observe.

Similarly, technologies such as AI are part of today's attempts to learn more about the unknown than our limited observations and minds can understand. With our algorithms, we attempt to divine truth from a mercurial world. We as humans create and use tech—such as hepatoscopy and artificial intelligence—to overcome our human limitations and learn as much as we can about the world. In a very real sense, both point to humanity's quest to become omniscient; to know all things as God knows all things. Our quest for omniscience says a great deal about our human nature—our thirst for knowledge and our desire to be on a level playing field with God.

If humanity knows all things, it can wage war with impunity. It can create tech that will allow us to extend life forever. It can journey to the farthest reaches of our universe. It can make us think we might actually be God.

To the mind of God, however, who stands outside of creation, our artificial intelligence is little more than examining livers.

MARJORIE PRIME
BRAIN-COMPUTER INTERFACE
AND THE NATURE OF PEOPLE

Jon: *Does it bother you that your mother is talking to a computer program, or that a computer program is pretending to be your dad?*

Tess: *It bothers me that you are helping it pretend to be some fountain of youth version of my dad.*

Jon: *It's how she remembers him. And she accepts it because it is clever.*

Tess: *Clever—like a mirror, like a backboard.*

Jon: *No, no, it's more than that. . . . It's like a child learning to talk, only it does it so quickly—that's how we think we're talking to a human. The more you talk, the more it absorbs, including our imperfections.*

[Later]

Tess: *You talked to Jon?*

Marjorie Prime: *He wants to help me be more real to help you. You've been so down.*

Tess: *Pity from a computer . . . it feels . . . Do you have emotions, Marjorie? Or do you just remember ours? Do you feel anything?*
Marjorie Prime: *I like to know more. It makes me better. More human.*
—*MARJORIE PRIME*

It was Jon's idea to get Walter Prime for Marjorie. After Walter's death, Marjorie had entered into a slow and downward spiral, drifting into the melancholic shadows of advanced age. Her son-in-law Jon thought having a prime would help Marjorie process her grief and offer her a respite from loneliness.

Tess, however, was not so sure. She wasn't sure that having a prime was a suitable option for her mother. Tess didn't seem to trust the technology behind primes; it felt cold and unnatural to her. Once Marjorie became comfortable with Walter Prime, however, it became a regular fixture of her life until she too succumbed to death.

After Marjorie passed, Jon also felt it wise to get Tess a Marjorie Prime in an attempt to help her with the grieving. It took time for Tess to warm up to the idea of a Marjorie Prime, just as it had with the Walter Prime. But having her mom as a prime soon helped. Tess had struggled to understand her mom when she was still living. In death, Tess was now able to understand her mom quite well.

A prime is a computer representation of a person. It can interact with other people in the same way that a computer can: either through a 2D interface (such as a computer screen today) or a 3D interface (such as a VR headset, augmented reality, or hologram in the near future). Primes are created by transferring the memories and personalities of a person into a virtual avatar. This allows for a kind of immortality. When Walter passed away, Jon had a prime created of him for Marjorie. And when Marjorie died, Jon had a prime created of her for Tess. When Tess passed away prematurely, Jon created a prime of her also—for himself and his grandkids.

Marjorie Prime, written for the screen, produced, and directed by Michael Almereyda and based on the play by Jordan Harrison, tells the story of four generations of a family coping with life and loss. In the midst of learning to live with death, the family's grieving process is augmented by the introduction of new technology: brain-computer interfaces, called primes.

An important subtext for *Marjorie Prime* is a reference to thoughts about how memory works from the philosopher William James: "Memory proper, or secondary memory as it might be styled, is the knowledge of a former state of mind after it has already once dropped from consciousness; or rather *it is the knowledge of an event, or fact,* of which meantime we have not been thinking, *with the additional consciousness that we have thought or experienced it before.*"[1]

In other words, we remember things that have passed beyond our immediate thoughts; in remembering these things, the recall of them actually recolors our memories. Therefore, the more times we remember something, the more coloration can occur.

Primes are not merely containers of unchangeable past information, however. As the primes interact, they learn and grow. Their knowledge and personality change and adapt to present information. Thus, when they tell stories from the past, over time these stories change based on human inputs.

Eventually these stories are not exactly history but a type of rewritten history for whomever will listen.

Marjorie, the adopted granddaughter of Jon and Tess, never knew in life her great-grandmother Marjorie, for whom she was named. But she did know Marjorie Prime, a replica of her great-grandmother, created by her grandparents. Marjorie Prime is an imperfect replica of the original Marjorie, based on a selective knowledge of Marjorie's life.

When we look back at our own pasts, do we know them completely or selectively? Does the more we know about the past help or hurt our future? Within a few generations, there will be the potential for millions of primes: virtual representations of people who have passed. As people's lives are increasingly uploaded to a computer, will it become a boon to society? Or will we become blasé about wandering through our own hall of ancestors? When memory is rewritten by a prime, whose version of the past should we trust? And what will the testimony of past generations mean for those living far into the future?

SAMPLE TECH: BRAIN-COMPUTER INTERFACE

A few years ago, my dad died. In the months that followed his funeral, my family had to sort out his belongings. In the collection of boxes allocated to me, I discovered one that contained personal keepsakes from my grandmother.

When my grandmother had died several decades before, my father just boxed up her stuff and put it in the attic. I suspected some of her keepsakes would be among his belongings—but I had no way of knowing what he kept and what he discarded. When I went through her stuff in my dad's box, I was saddened by the fact that there were only a very few things with which I could piece together her and my grandfather's lives. Ninety-nine percent of my grandmother's and grandfather's lives have been lost to time.

The only great find was a set of black and white negatives from around the 1920s. I was able to get these photos professionally scanned, and now a young version of my grandparents lives on in my digital photo display (protected on a RAID drive with multiple backups).[2]

Taking another step back, I know almost nothing about any of my great-grandparents. Except for their names and birthdates, their lives are entirely hidden from those of us who remain on earth. It's sad, in a way, that their stories—the challenges they faced and overcame—and their world has forever passed out of human knowledge. The goal of the brain-computer interface is to change that. If it were possible to upload consciousness to a computer, humanity would have achieved the first step toward living forever (not for our benefit, supposedly, but for the benefit of others). "Living forever" here suggests the limited sense of life extension, not "eternal life" as God defines it.

Compared to autonomous machines and gene editing, brain-computer interfaces seem a subtler technology. It's easy to imagine how autonomous machines and gene editing will change our world, for better and worse. It's harder to imagine how brain-computer interfaces will affect us. But more than any other near-future tech, brain-computer interfaces will change the way we define humanity.

Before we redefine humanity, though, let's start with a basic definition of this new tech. In the early twentieth century, scientists discovered that the brain produces electrical impulses that could be detected outside of the body.[3] With

the advent of computers—a system that understands electrical inputs—it seemed possible that one day, instead of using
a keyboard or computer mouse, someone could use the brain
as a means of input. What a wonderful world it would be
if I could delete website popups and self-starting ads with
my mind instead of having to manually nuke each one with
my mouse!

Neuroscientists Jonathan and Elizabeth Wolpaw explain
that there are several areas in which brain-computer interfaces
can change our world. First, they can assist those with disabili-
ties to have greater functionality; second, they can help people
do repetitive, manual tasks much more efficiently; third, they
can replace our less efficient interactions (such as our eternal
battle with pop-ups); and fourth, they can change the way we
interact with the world—the way we communicate with others, both in life and in death.[4] In another age, we would have
called it telepathy.

Even though a brain-computer interface may seem like
total science fiction, it is not; in fact, it has already arrived in
a limited form. Already these interfaces can help people with
missing limbs, spinal cord injuries, or Lou Gehrig's disease
to have greater communicative functionality, whether it be
on a computer or a remote-controlled device.[5] The primary
limitation of today's tech is that the person must literally plug
themselves into the computer every time they want to type an
email with their mind.[6]

Tech builds on past tech; you can't have autonomous
machines without first having assembly-line factories, and you
can't have assembly-line factories without first having metal
smelting. We won't have effective, wireless brain-computer
interfaces without these earlier plugged-in versions.

I already have a very rudimentary brain-computer interface; I call it a "digital camera."[7] With my eyes, I see my children playing in our yard. With my camera, I photograph them playing, and then I upload the photograph to my computer. The data point that I have captured with my camera was once a memory in my mind's eye; now it is a data point on a RAID drive. Because of the limitations of present technology, that data is both ephemeral and eternal.

I have about a dozen photos of my paternal grandparents, and a few dozen of my maternal grandparents. Their lives are almost beyond space and time and memory. But I don't just have a dozen photos of my kids; I have thousands. And I don't just have a birth certificate of my kids, as I do for one—and only one—of my grandparents; I have digital scans of their activities and achievements and some of their life stories. Today, it's easy to capture this information.

My documentation of my own children's lives is based on one of my biggest regrets. My maternal grandmother was a woman of significant faith. She lived a unique and meaningful life, even if it looked like nothing much from the world's perspective. When I was young and she'd start in on one of her fascinating stories, I'd always made a mental note that one day I would interview her and record her past. As I grew older, I always told myself, "I'll do it next time." Yet it never happened. My kids will never hear those stories. They are lost in the shadows of my own mind, irretrievable.

Right now we have a limited brain-computer interface. Much more powerful brain-computer interfaces are coming, such as whole brain emulation, in which we may be able to directly transfer the memories and perhaps even the personalities of people into a computer program. What we have now, compared to what is coming, is what the smoke signal was to the telegraph. The generations that follow will be able to know their ancestors in a way that we can only imagine. The impact on the psyche of our world will be greater than that of autonomous machines and gene editing combined. The reason is that technologies like autonomous machines and gene editing will primarily alter our culture and our biology, respectively, but brain-computer interfaces will alter our understanding of human nature, slowly but surely, from the inside out.

Here's where it gets weird. I'm not supposed to admit this in polite company, but my paternal grandmother had an interesting family tree. Though the details are erased by history, we know my father's grandfather Henry was born in 1844. I have one black-and-white photo of a person I believe to be my great-grandfather Henry. As a young man, he fought in the American Civil War, and then married a woman apparently much younger than himself. His grandson—my father—described Henry as a bit of a "scallywag" and "entrepreneur," though he never met him.

Could you imagine if Henry had had a digital camera? If he has posted his life to Facebook (which is just another rudimentary prototype of brain-computer interface)? If we look at Facebook now, we see people posting cringeworthy personal photos and even more cringeworthy political screeds. What a mess it would be to try to understand my great-grandfather's posts about his social views, or a photo of him with his probably too-young wife. And if we could have a prime of him— would I even let my kids get to know him? Cultural mores change so quickly, I suspect many of our ancestor's primes would be rated R.

PEOPLE, DEFINED

If a computer can capture my thoughts, my feelings, my memories, and even my personality, what makes me human? Are my disembodied thoughts, feelings, memories, and personality *me*? Or is my body me? Or are both me, but in a way that they can be separated? When I die, my body will go in the ground—but where will my soul go? Do I have a spirit and a soul, or just a soul? Does God's Spirit live in my body, or my soul, or both, or neither? If a computer can capture my thoughts, feelings, memories, and personality, is it capturing my soul or my spirit? Or is it just taking a "digital photo" of my soul at one point in time?

Here pushing the boundaries of tech forces us to confront age-old questions anew. There is one possible technological advancement that I await with bated breath—the head transplant of a human being. Some are quick to dismiss this as quackery, and it may be; but I also recognize that the idea of transplanting human body parts, such as hearts and kidneys, used to also be considered impossible and heterodox.[8] In the near future, we may harvest human organs grown inside of special pigs. If I have a heart grown in a pig, is it still mine? Or what if my mind is kept alive after my body dies—for days, weeks, or longer? Scientists have now accomplished this feat with pigs.[9] If one day scientists succeed in transplanting a human head—still an *if*, but not an unreasonable one—which person does the new person become? The one with the head, or the one with the body? And what happens when somebody tries to plant a "male" head on a deceased "female" body?

All these questions lead to the biggest one of all: What is a human being? Scholars of theology, ethics, medicine, neuroscience, and many other fields debate and write about this question extensively. This issue is too large for us to tackle here. But I am going to make one suggestion in this section, and one in the next, that are critical for our discussion of keeping faith in a world of limitless tech.

Here's how the prevailing story today goes: Through explainable and demonstrable physical processes, life took shape on our planet. Over the span of millions of years, simple life forms evolved into more complex life forms. These life forms share very similar genetic material, which lets us know how interrelated all living organisms are on our planet. About 140,000 years ago, give or take, most species that are prevalent today took shape.[10] Out of a number of competing hominins, including *Homo neanderthalensis* and *Homo floresiensis*, our species, *Homo sapiens*, emerged as the dominant species on the planet.

For the first 100,000 years of our species' existence, our dominance was not a foregone conclusion, as we lived in equilibrium with our world as hunter-gatherers. That style of existence came to halt once our ancestors discovered future tech in the form of agriculture. Once we became addicted to this new technology, we left hunting and gathering behind, our species began to grow in number, and we ended up in the biological driver's seat of planet Earth. As the dominant organic species today, we need to rethink how we live on our planet as we are affecting both the organic (e.g., extinction of other species) and inorganic (e.g., pollution).[11]

Notice how this prevailing story depicts a flattened world. There is no hint of the spiritual, only the material—we are matter composed of organic and inorganic molecules, nothing more. All of humanity's great works and ideas are essentially the result of biological progression. This doesn't mean that much of the prevailing story isn't true. What it means is that the prevailing story tries to explain who people are by excluding God and his work out of each part of this story. For example, we do need to think about our impact on our planet, but not because we are the dominant organic species. It is because God calls us to shepherd his world.

A great philosopher once sang, "You know that we are living in a material world, and I am a material girl."[12] This is an apt summary of the dominant worldview in which we find ourselves. I say "find ourselves" because as a Christian, I believe this world was created by God and that I am a spiritual sojourner in a world that is not really my own (see John 15:19; 1 Peter 2:11). Materialism—the idea that the physical world is all there is—flattens the world. But no matter how popular that prevailing worldview becomes, I know the world is much rounder than culture wants to admit. I know there is more to life than just the material, the organic and the inorganic.

This popular worldview presents Christians with an excellent opportunity to engage culture surrounding the question of what it means to be human. Many of the discussions about brain-computer interfaces, pigs' organs, and head transplants—at least as the media portrays them—treat human beings in strictly materialistic terms. Yet somewhere, deep inside everyone, is the sense that life is more than just the biological. We are created to know something greater is out there: a God who created us and wants to know us. We are also created knowing that there is something special about us; a soul inside us that helps us to live lives greater than the sum of our biological parts. As Christians, we understand all this quite well, in spiritual terms. As conversations increase about what it means to be human, we will have frequent opportunities to share this truth with the people we meet.

Here's an example. Everyone who knows me knows that I have a bit of a sweet tooth. I'm pretty much addicted to dark chocolate. But as I've gotten older, I eat more and more fruit, since I prefer naturally occurring sugars over processed sugars. Part of the reason is that some foods created today are highly addictive; the companies that produce them now have decades of experience in crafting food to which we can't say no. Dark chocolate and other candies have reached the pinnacle of this I-can't-say-no perfection. Almost anyone I talk to will quickly admit that there is some food out there they can't refuse.

Whenever we eat our guilty pleasure food, we keep eating and eating and eating. It seems like we can never get enough. This is the same way culture and technology work together in our lives. Apple and Google haven't made gazillions of dollars creating technology that is only moderately tempting to a few people, like a baby spinach and arugula salad. They make highly addictive tech that masses of consumers want. No matter how much tech (and culture) we get, though, it never fills us up. It never completes us. It never makes us satisfied.

That's because these things can never satisfy the basic longing that we all have—for something *more* to this life. And that something more is only made plain when the power of God gets ahold of our lives.

PEOPLE, REDEFINED

So what are human beings? Who are we? Why are we here in this material world?

We know from even a cursory reading of the Bible that humans are made in the "image of God" (see Genesis 1:26-27). Theologians have long debated what that idea of *imago*

Dei means, and there are several good explanations.[13] One possibility is that it suggests we are able to relate, to understand, to agree, and to love in the same way God can. Another possibility is that it implies we have access to qualities similar to those possessed by God, albeit in a much more limited form. I suspect that it is a concept with multiple meanings, rooted in the mystery of God, that we will not appreciate until sometime after we shuffle off this mortal coil.

Speaking of the mortal coil, this kind of sentiment was common in ages past but rarer today. For much of recorded history, the image of God was cast in nonmaterial concepts. The soul was of primary importance. In this sense, our soul was viewed as the seat of our relationship with God. Even though we will have a resurrection body (see 1 Corinthians 15:35-49), who we are was seen as rooted in our soul.[14]

The material and immaterial, the body and the soul: these make up a sort of pendulum for our understanding of human nature. Often in Christian history the pendulum has swung toward the immaterial—toward the soul. This makes sense when you live in a harsh world rife with death and famine. Holding onto the importance of the soul is necessary when you face an infant mortality rate like that of the late nineteenth century or in countries in the majority world.

Pendulums swing (as they always do), and the last century has seen an increase in focus among Christian thinkers on the significance of the physical body for defining a human being. We see this in popular theological discussions about "embodiment," citing the incarnation as a sort of proof that our physical form is a necessity. It is true that God created us with bodies, and that God sent Jesus in a body, and that as Christians we will be resurrected in physical bodies to live forever with God—in both a material and immaterial capacity. That's exciting to me, because the body is where experiences come from: with hands I touch, with eyes I see, with ears I hear, with nose I smell, with mouth I taste. The body is the interface that we have with our physical world; to paraphrase Paul, one day our heavenly body will be the physical interface that we have with our heavenly world (see 1 Corinthians 15:35-53).

Still, I believe the pendulum has swung too far toward the material. Just as we can overemphasize the soul, we can also overstate the importance of the body. I am not merely my body; I am more than my body. Though we do not well understand the journey through death's door, it seems that when I die there will be some type of separation or distinction between my material self and my immaterial self (see Romans 6:12, 7:24, 8:10; 1 Corinthians 6:17). Which of those selves will retain my essence the most? It seems the answer must be my immaterial self. If my body is in the ground, what does it retain?[15] Possibly something, but unless we deny the existence of the immaterial, that something would be secondary to what the soul retains. And if my body is the holy building in which my spirit dwells (see John 2:19-21; 1 Corinthians 6:19), should I not see the soul as primary and the body as secondary to who I am?

Isn't it God's Spirit, not merely the temple building (as finely created as it was), that made the temple God's dwelling place? Isn't it the people, not merely the church building (as finely crafted as it may be), that make the church?

Without going too deeply into theology here, it's possible for most people to perceive this shift from soul to body in Christian thought. Part of this wholesale shift toward materiality means we place greater emphasis on everything from the health of our planet, to the health and wealth of people, to the physical intimacy of married church members.

Here's why we need to start the pendulum back in the other direction: Christians must recover the importance of the soul. One reason is that there are areas of science trying to get rid of the soul.[16] There is no room for a soul in a flattened world— after all, there are only organics and inorganics. Strict materialism means there is nothing more than our physical bodies.

If we as Christians respond to the advances in science and technology by overemphasizing the body at the expense of the soul—which we have done—we have given up on the very evidence that there is an immaterial, spiritual part of life. As we support science and technology, we must also support the soul. We can appreciate one without denigrating the other.

Materialism is not a happy belief system. In my experience, most people, even most people who doubt the existence of God, don't want to be strict materialists. They still want to believe in *something*. Often they want to be spiritual—as they define it—without being religious. Or they want to write their own story that borders on what philosophers would call a mythology.

As future tech arrives, the culture that comes with it will be increasingly materialistic. Most people will be hungry for spiritual alternatives. We as the church can stand ready with a proven alternative—if we can recapture the importance of the soul.

Transhumanist thought will trump Christian thought if we make materiality our point of focus. In the face of future tech, the body becomes the focus of what great living looks like. It is a future in which we can more and more easily swap out broken parts, as if the human body were a machine such as a car or vacuum cleaner. Already today we have someone living with five organ transplants.[17] In the transhumanist ideal, if we can only replace enough body parts or create a powerful enough brain-computer interface, we can live forever. At that point, who needs a resurrection?[18]

THE BIBLICAL CENTAUR

The turning point between a past of agriculture and industry and a future of limitless tech may have been a chess game some twenty years ago. Way back in May 1997, IBM's Deep Blue computer defeated the human world champion Garry Kasparov in a standard, six-game match.[19] This set off a chain reaction of debate, both about the match itself and about how computers can and should compete with humans. It also opened up new avenues for play, with computers taking aim at other games and humans rethinking classic games in a quest to defeat digital logic.

Even though I don't follow the world of chess, I was aware of Garry Kasparov, Deep Blue, and much of the subsequent back and forth in the past two decades. I knew that we lived in a world of not just one type of chess player—human grandmasters—but two types of chess players—human grandmasters and intelligent supercomputers. What I didn't know is that we actually now live in a world with three types of chess players—humans, AIs, and centaurs.

In myth and legend, centaurs are creatures with the head, chest, and arms of a human and the legs and body of a horse. In chess, a centaur is a human player who plays alongside an AI against other centaurs, or single humans, or single supercomputers.[20] In this scenario, the human is the team leader, with the AI fulfilling an advisory role. For tech enthusiasts, centaurs are another sign of the coming evolution of people, one step forward in the human-machine hybrid. It is also another step toward the coming brain-computer interface.

Analogies that combine the Bible and sci-fi have very short shelf lives, but there is a metaphor here nevertheless. Just as we are starting to realize that humans powered by AI are successful at chess, so too have we known since the dawn of time that humans powered by God's wisdom are "successful" at life.[21] We can base this latter kind of hybrid on our divinely imaged humanity with access to God's truth: our perception of a Creator from our investigation of the world around us, and the Bible, which contains the message of God, coupled with two thousand years of Christian thought and argumentation at our fingertips.[22] The "AI" we have is God's Word and God's Spirit, which will guide us into truth no matter the changes in culture and technology. Christians have been "doing hybrid" for a long time. Braving the future will simply require us to be more skilled "centaurs" than ever before.

This brings us to a growing problem: How do we access and use God's truth the further out technology advances? This is not easy to answer.

As our world continues to evolve, we increasingly face issues that the Bible does not address directly. We must discern God's dream for the world with regard to everything from industrialization to macroeconomics to astrophysics; from transistor radios to vapes to nanoprobes. As we've seen, even basic ideas—about who we are as human beings and our role in the universe—are undergoing primary shifts that necessitate a better understanding of humanity from God's perspective.[23] And in turn, this will require clearer notions of who God is and what God's role is in our everyday lives.

In ages past, a casual reading of Scripture seemed enough to handle many situations.[24] This is no longer the case. Instead, the faster the world evolves, the harder it becomes to extrapolate biblical truths into daily situations. Therefore, in a world of limitless tech, the more precise our interpretation of the Bible must become and the more diligently we need to study its pages and its history. For all the work the church has done, it must work harder if it will have any ability to speak into a future world.

Future tech such as the brain-computer interface will allow humanity to expand further than it ever dreamed. With access to unlimited resources, we will become our own primes, who will live for near-eternity in a digital state.

Indeed, our lives are already being recorded to such a large degree that we should pause to ask ourselves: Who will our future self be? Will our prime be one of surface successes—such as the typical Facebook profile or Marjorie in *Marjorie Prime*? Or will our lives proclaim the good news of Christ until his return?

OMNIPRESENCE

One day, when I am long gone, my kids will be able to open up a 2D compilation of my life that they can show my grandkids. One day, when my kids are long gone, my grandkids will be able to open 3D holograms of their parents that will speak to my grandkids about their parents' lives. One day when my grandkids are long gone, my great-grandkids will be able to show an avatar of their parents to my great-great-grandkids. And one day when all these descendants of mine are long gone, their descendants will interact with the thoughts and feelings of my descendants in a way that we today cannot imagine.

Each of these progressive evolutions in brain-computer interfaces demonstrate that we are closing in on a point where we can be at any place and any time into the future. It will appear to our descendants that humanity will have achieved a certain type of immortality by connecting their words, their photos, their ideas, their feelings, and eventually maybe even their brain scans to a computer interface.

This will quickly give humanity the impression of omnipresence: the sense that we can be everywhere at any time. Even today, in our increasingly interconnected global village, I can be virtually present in many locations in the same day. Only a century ago, the vast communicative power individual people enjoy today would have seemed king-like, if not godlike.

One of the first things we learn as children, through song and rhyme, is that "God is great." And God *is* great, both in character and magnitude. God is immense—greater than anything we can know or understand. Our universe is not in any way comparable to a grain of sand on a seashore of God's immense nature. This unique aspect of God necessitates that he will be omnipresent in our world.

This means God will always be everywhere in both space and time. It is not simply that God is with me when I am going about my day; God is present in all times past and present, for all people, for all creation, in every way. This gives God an ultimate freedom that we can never know or understand, as we are always fully limited by both space and time.[25]

One reason we can never replace God—even if one day we unite with computers and can exist in all relevant places—is that we cannot exist in all times. We cannot peer back in time and uncover all the first causes for anything in our world. Without those, we will never be able to solve longstanding problems in our world such as evil, sin, and selfishness—problems that only God can solve.[26]

There's a little more to it than this, and the psalmist captures the breadth of these ideas remarkably well:

> Where can I go from your Spirit? Where can I flee from your presence?
>
> If I go up to the heavens, you are there; if I make my bed in the depths, you are there.
>
> If I rise on the wings of the dawn, if I settle on the far side of the sea, even there your hand will guide me, your right hand will hold me fast.
>
> If I say, "Surely the darkness will hide me and the light become night around me," even the darkness will not be dark to you; the night will shine like the day, for darkness is as light to you. (Psalm 139:7-12)

God is not simply present in all places and times. God's sovereignty will work in all places and times. As Karl Barth noted, God's omnipresence is a great indicator of God's love for creation. God is in our business like no one else because he loves his creation.[27]

Marjorie Prime was available to her descendants because of their ability to access her when they wanted to. God is unlike a prime because we don't choose to access God; God chooses to access us. What a privilege it is to be accessed by our Creator.

CHARIOT OF FIRE

When it comes to future tech, the coolest book in the Bible is undoubtedly Ezekiel. Like many Christians, I used to find Ezekiel hard to understand and a wee bit strange—for example, all the moving wheels intersecting each other (see Ezekiel 1:15-21). As a biblical scholar, I still find Ezekiel hard to understand and more than a wee bit strange, but I have also had the pleasure of learning a little about its cultural and historical background.

Let's agree with all the tin-foil hat-wearers and UFO hunters on the internet for a second and assume that the wheels in Ezekiel are representative of a future tech. But the future tech it represents is the chariot, not some kind of alien spaceship. Even more than the composite bow, the chariot in the ancient world was a technology that was also a formidable weapon. Chariots could change the balance of power for any king who possessed them. A chariot was the ultimate symbol of both power and presence. It's no wonder that early depictions of God—like those discovered recently in Israel—use the chariot as a way of expressing God's immensity.[28]

The chariot symbolized the king's ability to be anywhere at any time. For Ezekiel, the chariot was the power of God to be anywhere at any time. It was often associated with God's presence in the temple—the place God dwelled on Earth. These archaeological discoveries not only depict God, the temple, and the chariot, but show them in interaction with each other. They show God dwelling in the temple but with a chariot at his command, giving God the ability to move to and fro—in any direction—through the world.

Ezekiel depicts this symbolically in the first chapter of his book. After describing these chariots, he explains, "And when the living creatures went, the wheels went beside them; and when the living creatures rose from the earth, the wheels rose. Wherever the spirit wanted to go, they went, and the wheels rose along with them, for the spirit of the living creatures was in the wheels" (Ezekiel 1:19-20 ESV).

In this magnificent vision, God is seated on the throne, surrounded by living creatures who reveal God's glory. The way the chariots worked is that "the divine spirit that controlled the beings' wings in flight also controlled the wheels on the ground and kept them attached when the apparatus was airborne. The whole was an extension of the omnipresent spirit."[29] God's omnipresence is the demonstration of God's power from the throne room through every inch of creation.

Future tech, such as virtual reality and brain-computer interface, will greatly extend our presence in time and space. But it will never complete humanity's quest to be like God. We may be able to one day plug ourselves into the mainframe, but we'd be better served to plug ourselves into God. There is simply no *where* or *when* in which God is not present.

ROBOT & FRANK
INTELLIGENT ROBOTS AND
THE POWER OF STORY

*The robot is not your servant, Maddie. You don't turn him on
and off! Like he's a slave! . . . It's not you, it's not you. I need
him. I do . . . . You don't understand. I need him. He's my friend.*
—FRANK, *ROBOT & FRANK*

One day Frank had a marvelous idea. A marvelous, stupen-
dous, could-it-really-be-possible idea. Could the robot help
Frank pick a lock? Could the robot help Frank enter back into
his old life as a successful jewel thief?

Frank was retired, comfortably, so he didn't need the
money. He had quit at the top of his game. Frank was a good
jewel thief. So, no, this urge was more about finding comfort
in work that one was good at. It was about remembering one's
purpose in life—that, and boredom, as Frank seemed to be
in a fog many days. Could the robot really help him? Could
it be trained to do something its programmers never thought

possible? Most importantly, could it keep all these new activities a secret?

The robot in *Robot & Frank* is an ideal robot helper. It is quiet and unobtrusive; it only volunteers to help when its programming suggests it is reasonable to do so. It is uncharacteristically passive by human standards. It is also not very human, as it never intentionally interferes with human activity. This was part of the reason that Frank's son Hunter thought it a good idea to get the robot for his dad—to give him additional companionship in the last years of Frank's life. Frank's daughter Madison was less convinced, having moral objections to the use of intelligent robots. Frank struggled with dementia, and he needed additional support—something that the robot was able to provide and his family was not.

Robot & Frank, based on a screenplay by Christopher Ford, tells the story of how an intelligent robot integrates into the life of a retiree. At first, Frank is put off by the robot; over time, he not only accepts the robot but starts to treat the robot as a kind of person.

Nothing says "science fiction" like an intelligent robot. We've seen them in countless movies, from Gort in *The Day the Earth Stood Still* to Ultron in the *Avengers*. But the robots that we are likely to encounter in the near future will be nothing like Gort or Ultron—they will be more like the robot in *Robot & Frank*. They will be quiet, unassuming robots who are "off" except when assisting people in their day-to-day tasks—someone (er . . . some*thing*) that will take out the trash or sort the recycling without grumbling.

Intelligent robots in our homes may seem hard to imagine. This is because in our minds they are close to flying cars—a tech long promised but never delivered. Likely we will go through several generations of robots, with the first few generations functioning like the "portable" phones of the 1980s did: not well.

Yet the coming wave of intelligent robots will create a number of crucial questions. To what use and purposes should people use intelligent robots? How do we prevent intelligent robots from being (unintentionally) destructive? How should we treat our intelligent robots? Is it possible to "abuse" a robot? These are just the tip of the proverbial iceberg. In the end, our answers will say much more about us, as humans, than about our metallic helpers.

SAMPLE TECH: INTELLIGENT ROBOT

Let's start with a basic definition: An intelligent robot is any device that can move and think (in some capacity).[1] Put another way, an intelligent robot is essentially an autonomous machine with some artificial general intelligence mixed in. Like all the future tech we have surveyed so far, intelligent robots are both here already and coming soon. Yet they are still in a stage of early infancy, and for the most part they exist only as prototypes.

From self-driving lawnmowers (autonomous machines) to the *Avalon*'s Arthur (artificial intelligence) to Frank's robot (intelligent robot), exact definitions can seem a bit fluid. Using my categories here, the difference between each of these three examples is how their intelligence relates to their mechanical processes. I categorize the lawnmower as an autonomous machine because its designers created it to do one thing and to do that one thing well, both mechanically and in its algorithmic AI. Arthur is an example of the preliminary use of narrow AI, because it has a Siri-like ability to interact with humans. But its mechanical ability is very limited, as it runs on a track and does only a few things well. In some ways, Arthur is closer to the lawnmower than it is to Frank's robot. Frank's robot is the start of a truly intelligent robot, as it has the most advanced AI and greater mechanical function than the previous examples— neither the lawnmower nor Arthur can go pick a lock and steal a jewel or whatever other task their owner could imagine.

Much like autonomous machines and AI, intelligent robots will rapidly proliferate as these other technologies improve. The time is coming when, along with an automobile, an HDTV, and a smartphone, most middle-class Westerners will have an intelligent robot. When this occurs, the resulting revolutions in society will be as great as those caused by the clepsydra, the capacitor, the internet, or the smartphone.[2]

One ancient tech I have been using recently is the kayak. Growing up near a small pond in Virginia, I have always been fascinated by the water. During adolescence one of my favorite activities was waterskiing. As I got older, I had a chance to try kayaking in exotic places like Hawaii and Alaska. When my family and I moved to South Carolina, there was a lake near our house, so I bought a used kayak.

When I am out on the lake, I am transported to a world where the evidence of God seems far more palpable. For me, it is easier to see it in the visceral aesthetics of nature than in the brick and mortar of human industry. On the lake, there is ample evidence of God's creative work. As I paddle the rippled, brown-glass surface of the lake, under the blue- and red-hued skies created by the setting sun, I pass over hundreds of bubbles emerging from the fish and lake life below. When I paddle in the shallows I often dredge up lake weeds, and by the bank I can see the family of geese and one of the herons that live on the lake. It's a perfect microcosm of the world as I understand it.

Our culture's perception of that world is changing. With the ways we speak and how we live, it is being flattened into mere materialism; animals and earth, organics and inorganics. In that world there is no mystery or revelation; it is more malleable (and in many ways, exploitable) than ever before. Will intelligent robots think of beauty, or will they will think only of resources? What will happen when intelligent robots start to become a regular part of human society? What will happen when they interact with our world? I predict two things.

First, intelligent robots will, over time, start to seem "human" to us. Expect robot manufacturers to make them look human. The greater intelligence and mobility they have, the more likely humans will react to them as if they are some sort of people. The greater their intelligence and mobility, the more they will affect us.[3]

A look at Western culture is instructive. We have house pets that we have named, housed, fed, watered, and in some cases, clothed. We talk to our dogs and cats, and we believe they understand us. For example, when I am thinking about who God is or what the Bible says, and my cat, Sitka, comes over, I share my thoughts with him in a way that makes me feel as though he understands. Of course, he doesn't, but that doesn't stop me. (As I tell my kids, I love my cat, but if the roles were reversed, he'd probably just eat me.) As human beings, there is something about our being made in the image of God that makes us quick to attribute essence, personality, and souls to nonhuman creatures and things.

The more humanlike intelligent robots appear, the more tempting it will be for humans to treat them as persons. And the more humans treat intelligent robots as persons, the greater the demand will be for these robots to appear human. Once they show up in our homes, we will house, feed, water, clothe, and yes, name them. They will become person-like—human-*ish*, if you will.

Second, most humans will treat intelligent robots like property. This may seem noncontroversial, at first blush. After all, what is wrong with treating mechanical constructions like property?

A robot is, in essence, a complex machine designed by humans. We have other complex machines, such as washing machines and automobiles. A washing machine is my property; I bought it, and I can use it—or abuse it—as I see fit. And then I can throw it away. No one would think there was anything unusual about that. But if I treated an animal such as a dog or cat that way, there would be an outcry—and rightfully so.

The difference between an intelligent robot and a washing machine is likely to be huge. People don't name washing machines. Washing machines don't watch your kids, listen to your stories, give you advice, or laugh at your jokes. People make cats into "persons" because they respond to us; they watch our kids, listen to our stories, give us advice (we like to believe), and laugh at our jokes (they do). Even more than pets, intelligent robots will respond in all those ways also—and in a language that we can understand.

In both a traditional Western as well as an orthodox Christian worldview, people have souls. Do robots have souls? Our kneejerk response is likely no, absolutely not! But what is a soul? Our Creator imbued us with a soul that makes us something greater than our flesh-and-blood parts. Though the Bible never defines "soul," it refers to it frequently. From this we get the idea that a soul is the essence of a creature; it is the breath of life that comes from God that animates all that we are and do (see 1 Corinthians 15:45; Acts 17:28). What if we create a robot with something that seems a little greater to us than its metal and wire parts? What if we create a robot that believes it has a soul? Is it possible to create a robot with a soul?

I am not arguing that robots will have souls in the way people have souls. But because we as people are attempting to spark life into metal, in a sense that is not that dissimilar from God breathing life into dust (see Genesis 2:7), I am simply arguing that it is going to get confusing.[4] And worse.

In the future, we will react to intelligent robots as some type of persons, especially the more humanlike they appear. We will also view them as property. We will hear of people who buy nice, friendly, personable robots—and who make those robots do horrible things. We will see people mistreat and abuse robots.[5] And we will feel sorrow for those robots, because those robots will be like our robots. In the end, we will create a slave class. As this occurs, it will speak volumes about our humanity.

In the future, there will be organics and inorganics, and robots are inorganic. They are not worthy of status, but they will become objects of sympathy. The whole point of creating intelligent robots should be to help people, not create jewel thieves or to suffer abuse at the hands of human beings. Yet already there is a move to create robots that will offer humans an outlet for criminal or antisocial behavior.[6] The question is not just how we want to be treated by robots. It's how should we treat robots, and whether how we treat robots will begin to affect how we treat other people.[7]

In a famous line from *Star Wars*, Wuher, the cantina bar-tender at Mos Eisely spaceport on Tatooine, tells Luke, "We don't serve their kind here," referring to Luke's droids. In the future, we won't serve their kind either; they will serve us. This evolution in our society will lead us to believe that all power is invested in us, that there is nothing human ingenuity cannot do.

TRANSHUMANISM

Social evolution brings widespread change, and one that is on the near horizon is transhumanism. This worldview already appears regularly in certain cultural contexts, such as in the scripts of Hollywood movies and on the lips of tech titans in Silicon Valley (even if it's not explicitly named as such). Future tech arrives with certain cultural expectations built in through the marketing and distribution of the tech, one of which will be the transhuman ideal. Up to this point we have been describing transhumanism in general terms; here we have the opportunity to dig a little deeper.

As a starting point, consider the term *transhuman*. The *trans* part of the word stands for "transitional." What this means is that a transhuman represents the transition from human to posthuman.[8]

Human → Transhuman → Posthuman

In other words, today we are human; what our species will become, in the next evolutionary leap in the far future, is something posthuman. Somewhere between our human past and our posthuman future, we will start to transition. Transhumanists believe we are on the verge of starting this transition; we are becoming transhuman.

Being "human," in the above chart, does not mean simply living as people here on Earth, of a kind different than orangutans, elands, turnips, or radishes. Instead it refers to an idea about the place and purpose of humanity; it is a worldview called *humanism*. Humanism is a broad idea, with a complicated history, but one that we need to come to terms with if we want to understand "transitional humanism."[9]

Humanism (in its modern sense) started more than six hundred years ago, with the rediscovery in Europe of ancient Greek culture.[10] With ties to the Renaissance, humanism was at first a movement that encouraged the beauty and goodness of human accomplishment. In a century or so, this led to humanism emphasizing the importance of building up humanity—and individuals—through education and the arts. After a few more centuries, humanism started to move toward focusing on the goodness of humanity apart from God. In the past century or two, this has been the main idea behind humanism. Definitions of humanism include "a set of presuppositions that assigns to human beings a special position in the scheme of things" and "a non-religious, non-theistic, and naturalistic approach to life."[11]

In other words, humanism today sees humanity, not God, as seated on the throne of our world. In its most common contemporary form, humanism stands in direct competition with biblical ideas about who God is, why people exist, and what people's purposes are. We might also say that a "hard" version of humanism evolved from a "soft" version of humanism during the Renaissance. The "soft" form—a love for humanity—gave way to the "hard" form—a worship of humanity.[12]

One idea to note: in humanist thought, there has long existed the idea that the more we improve humanity, the more humanity would grow and change and reach its fullest potential. After Darwin, this change was often cast into evolutionary terminology: the goal of humanism is for humans to evolve into the next phase of humanity.

This is where transhumanism comes in. Transhumanists believe that technology will be the catalyst that starts our evolutionary leap toward becoming posthuman. One political scientist suggests, "Transhumanists argue not only that modern science and technology are giving human beings the power to take evolution into our own hands to improve the human species, and then to create some new species entirely, but also the ability to improve on all of nature. Much like the older apocalyptic visions, the transhumanists believe that mankind as we know it and nature as we know it are on their way out . . . [they believe] we *must* redesign humanity so that our ruinous flaws can be eliminated."[13]

Thus, if we want to eliminate the flaws in people, and the problems in our world, technology will give us the power to finally achieve these things.

Just as humanism is a broad and complex idea, so too is transhumanism. At present, there appear to be two versions of transhumanism that we may encounter—a "soft" version and a "hard" version—like we saw in humanism.[14] In the soft form, transhumanists focus on creating technology with the goal of improving human life. This is the kind of transhumanism echoed most in popular culture.[15] In the hard form, transhumanists see themselves at odds with Christianity in that they desire to create technology that forces humanity to evolve into the gods of our universe. This is the kind of transhumanism that we find in seminars and books by a number of self-identified transhumanist thinkers.[16]

Several technological planks comprise the foundation for transhumanism. These planks include a general human improvement (expanding human knowledge and abilities in a global context); superintelligent, general AI (multiplying the speed of our technological advancement faster than humans are capable of without computer assistance); body enhancement (adding to our physical form to help us better navigate our world); radical life extension (advancing medicine so that the life expectancy is in the hundreds of years); and cognitive immortality (transferring our minds to computer systems so that we may live forever). Typically, the "harder" the form of transhumanism, the greater the force adherents maintain should be applied to set up these planks in our society. Either way, these are the building blocks to our evolutionary escape. Expect to see culture trumpet these ideas in the near future.

Sometimes this topic of transhumanism seems weird or obscure to people. Often when I mention the word *transhumanism* in day-to-day conversation, I get blank stares. It seems divorced from the real world. Yet culture seeds the idea that humanity will triumph over its limitations if it can merely embrace the power of technology. This transhumanist idea affects everyone, whether we realize it or not.

Technology is a wonderful tool that allows us as humans to improve our lives. This fact might seem to make technology an extension of God's original plan. Yet technology is not a tool that can empower us to be gods, nor can it save humanity.

A NEW RELIGIOUS MOVEMENT?

If you are reading this and beginning to think that transhumanism sounds sort of like a religion, well, you wouldn't be wrong. Even though many strains of transhumanism reject

God and traditional forms of religion, virtually all transhumanist ideas originated within a Western Christian worldview. Remember, humanism started with a recognition of human achievement and flourishing and then evolved into a worship of humanity. Similarly, transhumanism starts with a recognition of the transformative power of new tech within human achievement. It then evolves into an empowerment of humanity over and above gods.

If transhumanism sounds religious, and it has adherents who see it as a new type of religion, should we consider it a new religious movement?[17] No, not really, at least at this point. Consider it more like a human idea sometimes taken to extremes.

Humanism and transhumanism are both better understood as troublesome parts of what it means to be intelligent creatures in a broken world. We live in a world of isms. An ism is any idea that started small, in a compelling way, and over time expanded into a comprehensive idea that purports to explain large swaths of human existence. Isms often attract followers—sometimes worshipers—in ways that reveal more about the nature of people than they do about the validity of the ism.

We encounter isms of all stripes and colors in our world today: capitalism, communism, feudalism, supralapsarianism, socialism, Calvinism, deism, UFOism, secularism, nationalism, and thousands more. These worldviews are like umbrellas that protect a set of ideas. I find it a peculiar part of human nature that people feel comfortable when they have an umbrella under which their views about the world can exist.

Ferris Bueller, in the eponymous movie *Ferris Bueller's Day Off*, said it best: "Isms, in my opinion, are not good. A person should not believe in an ism, he should believe in himself." The irony, of course, as readers of this book are already aware, is that Ferris is promoting an ism—humanism—without realiz ing it. Unfortunately, there is no escaping isms in our world. Isms are human systems. Because they are human systems, they are flawed—sometimes terribly flawed.

Humanism and transhumanism, like capitalism, Calvinism, and most other isms, have some good points and some bad points. Humanism brings with it a number of meaningful strengths (such as encouraging respect for other humans and promoting the value of education and arts). But a person can also be so humanistic that she or he dismisses God (a branch of humanism that is often referred to as secular humanism). Someone may ask, "A biblical worldview has respect for other humans and values education and the arts, for example; so why not dispense with humanism entirely?" That's a good point, and I sympathize with this thinking. But as I noted above, it is hard to be in a world with humans and not have to deal with human systems. To make the contrast by way of another great philosopher from the 1980s: heaven is *not* a place on earth—heaven is a place without isms.[18] In heaven we won't need umbrella ideas because God's glory will be our umbrella (see Revelation 21:1-4, 22-27). We won't need human systems because God's divine person will be the system.

This discussion naturally leads to the question "How should Christians respond to transhumanism?" Just the term alone will probably cause a knee-jerk negative reaction among sections of Christianity. Some Christians will assume the two are incompatible, just as they assume that science is incompat ible with faith.[19]

I would argue that transhumanism is in a similar range of compatibility with Christian theology as capitalism or humanism is. Treating transhumanism well—as I believe the church should also treat capitalism and humanism—would mean taking it with a big grain of salt. Responding faithfully to transhumanism will require sticking closely to biblical principles, the example of Christ, the tradition of the church, and the inspiration of the Spirit as discerned in Christian community.

In the end, if we are sure to understand and articulate the limitations in all human systems, there is no definitive biblical or theological reason to reject transhumanism as a whole.[20] In fact, if we engage transhumanists well, we may find over time that transhumanist advocates are more receptive to biblical viewpoints than those who have embraced past isms that have held sway in our world.[21]

That will be the hard part of braving the future: living in creative contact with worldviews with substantial differences to our own in a way that speaks into those worldviews. If ancient Christians could speak into the isms of their day, which included Neoplatonism and Caesarism, then near-future Christians can and will speak into transhumanism, to the glory of God.

ONE STORY (OR ANOTHER)

Nothing can move the human soul like a story. Nothing can instruct and teach like a well-crafted narrative. One of the most powerful forces in our universe is story, and one of the most powerful forms of story is found today in movies. For people living in the early twenty-first century, moviemaking tends to be the ultimate form of storytelling.

Let's consider a tale of four stories, then.

The first one is J.R.R. Tolkien's *The Lord of the Rings*, adapted for the big screen by Peter Jackson. Jackson's version wasn't perfect, but it probably captured the power of Tolkien's story as well as film could. It's an epic and rich story with plenty of movie magic thrown in.

The second one is George Lucas's *Star Wars*. Like *The Lord of the Rings*, *Star Wars* is one of the most famous movies of all time. *Star Wars* has captivated audiences and even spawned a new religious movement, Jediism. It accomplished all of this with weak dialogue in parts and inconsistencies here and there. Lucas built his story world with structural ideas from the works of Joseph Campbell, a professor of literature who studied mythology. What *Star Wars* may have lacked in storytelling details, it made up for in special effects. *Star Wars* is no *Lord of the Rings*, but it is still a great story and movie.

The third one is James Cameron's *Avatar*. This movie is the highest-grossing movie of all time, and for good reason. I saw it at the IMAX in 3D the week it came out, and the visual images were above and beyond anything that I have ever seen. Yet with the clichés, the unsurprising story arc, and the filler scenes, the story of *Avatar* left a lot to be desired. After the special effects wore off in my imagination after a day or so, my mind began processing the story behind the movie. It became clear to me pretty quickly that without the special effects, the movie would probably have been a dud. The story itself just wasn't that good.

All three of these movies made bazillions of dollars by communicating their stories at the box office. Note the differences, however: one had remarkable storytelling with great visuals and good special effects; one had very good storytelling with awesome special effects; and one had meh storytelling with amazing special effects.

Even if you disagree with my film critique, here is the point: special effects—typically achieved through tech—can make storytelling better. And in the case of *Avatar*, tech can obscure bad storytelling and make the story more meaningful than it would be otherwise.

I bet you thought I forgot the fourth story, but I didn't. You're familiar with it. It's the greatest story ever told. It is the good news—the best news ever, actually:

> Once there was a great God who loved people who were made in his image. In time, the creation rebelled, resulting in their alienation from God and each other. Yet this great God still loved people enough to make a way to rescue them from their rebellion. The way that God did this was to send his Son into creation to serve as a mediator between God and people. God's Son, Jesus, lived among people to share the good news of what God was doing and to show people how they should live. Because of people's rebellion, many could not understand how God was working. At the hands of people, God's Son was executed, even though he was innocent. In so doing, his innocent blood was sprinkled on the lives of those willing to commit to him. Showing that even death could not stop him, Jesus returned to life and soon after ascended back to God. With this, people understood that God defeated death and evil, making a way to reconcile people back to himself. People could be rescued from their rebellion! For those God rescues—they will die, but will one day live again in new bodies, in the same place where God dwells.[22]

That is the greatest story ever. When we share that story with others, a lot of people decide that they are not going in the right direction and they need a course correction.

When Jesus lived on earth, he told this same story (as well as others) in a variety of ways. Jesus even used special effects.

We often call them "miracles." He used special effects to rein-force the story he told in order to get his audiences' attention.[23]

There is one other story that I failed to mention in my earlier list. And it is one that most people have not heard very often at this point. This emerging story goes something like this:

> On the third planet in a solar system on the edge of a non-descript arm of a nondescript galaxy in the vast universe, conditions slowly became favorable for life. After billions of years, life began to evolve. Over time, increasingly com-plex life forms fought their way to the top of the biological heap, only to be supplanted by newer and more complex life forms. At some point, more than 100,000 years ago, one species evolved to a point where it would exercise dominance over all other species: *Homo sapiens*. *Homo sapiens* were themselves a product of the natural selection of numerous hominin species. Since coming to dominance, *Homo sapiens* has continued to evolve not just biologically but technologically. From stone chisels to the wheel to sat-ellites to spaceships, *Homo sapiens* headed down the track to become something so much greater.
>
> If humans can pull together, they can use technology to cre-ate a world of their dreams. In that future there is no more sadness, or tears, for the old species has passed away. They will be a new species enjoying life forever on their planet, or maybe even among the stars beyond.[24]

My point in all this is simple: Transhumanists have a story, just like Christians do. The transhumanist story is a pretty powerful one, and it will resonate with a lot of people on our planet.[25] The transhumanist story is a lot better than *Avatar*'s, that's for certain. It's probably on the level of *Star Wars*. It will prove at least as seductive as humanism, and maybe more so.

As Christians, we can be confident that our story is better and more accurate and more deeply true. But we must not assume that transhumanism doesn't have a compelling story. The transhumanist story will be just deceptive enough to lead people away from the central truth of our universe—that there is a God who loves us and who has a plan for our lives.

Should we worry about the religion of transhumanism? No.
Should we worry about the story of transhumanism? Yes.

OMNIPOTENCE

A hallmark of the modern American educational system is the science fair. Though I liked science in high school, I loathed having to create an "experiment" for my school's annual science fair. Now, as a parent of young children, I look forward to loathing it in a whole new way in a few years.

My first year competing in the mandatory science fair yielded a transistor radio I made myself from parts from a science fair kit that could be mail ordered with instructions. It was a bit shabby and didn't work so well. The student next to me had one of those baking-soda-and-vinegar volcanoes. Every science fair at every school since the dawn of time has had one of those, I am sure.[26]

The following year, with a great deal of Greek tragedy–like father-son conflict—including arguments over schematics from *Popular Science* and fights over whose turn it was to wind the coil—he and I built a large, working Tesla coil mounted on PVC pipe and plywood. Even if you've never seen a Tesla coil before, you probably know what it is—one of those towers that shoot lightning. Once my coil was working, it was truly amazing to touch the lightning with a rod and feel the high-voltage, low-amperage current course through your body and smell the bitter, oxidized air. I remember taking my four-foot, copper-colored coil to school, setting it up on the table where my name was, and plugging it in. DZZZZZZTTTT!!! The sound and fury of its powerful display held sway over anyone entering the gym. Best of all, no one was electrocuted.

If you think about it, a golden pillar that shoots lightning is pretty symbolic of power. My science fair project that year was literally powerful, at least in terms of the voltage generated. But my Tesla coil was powerful in another way. When I turned it on, everyone in the room stopped what they were doing. As a form of "advanced technology," it had a power over people in a way that is not easy to put into words.

Technology is powerful, and God is powerful, but they are not powerful in the same way. God and technology are, in fact, not at all similar when it comes to power.

When we describe God's power, we say that God is almighty—that he has omnipotence. In some ways, God's omnipotence is the easiest attribute of God to understand: it essentially means that God can do anything. Yet God's omnipotence is not simply the potential for power; it is actually power realized. It is power in action. The theologian T. F. Torrance explains it this way: "We must reject all abstract notions of divine omnipotence, for omnipotence is not to be understood in terms of what we think God can do, defining it as potence raised to the nth power, i.e., as omni-potence, but in terms of what God actually is and actually has done. Thus we do not define God by omnipotence but define omnipotence by the Nature and Being of God as he has revealed himself to us in his creative and redemptive activity."[27]

Therefore, it doesn't do much good to speak of God as having the power to do something. This is only an implication of God-ness. Instead, we speak of God's power by virtue of what God has already accomplished. God's actions (such as creating the universe and loving people even though they are unrighteous) reveal his great power.

One way to look at God's omnipotence is through the lens of his holiness. God is holy, and contrary to popular Christian understanding, God's holiness doesn't have to do with God's distinctiveness as much as it has to do with his completeness. When we say God is one, or God is holy, we are also saying that God is almighty, because it is in his nature. God's power is in who he is, whereas a human's power is in what he or she can do.[28]

This brings us to the power of tech. The power of technology is in its potential, not in its actuality (the way God's power is). If I want to cut down a tree, I can use modern tech such as an axe, or even more modern tech such as a chainsaw, and it is possible for me to cut down a tree. These technologies are tools that I choose to use or not use. It is also possible for me to cut down a tree without an axe or a chainsaw, just me with my bare hands. Yes, it would take me a really long time, and it would hurt a lot, depending on the size of the tree. The point is threefold: I as a human being have the potential to do things. Tech, such as axes and chainsaws, amplifies my potential. Yet all that God does and will do is already actually done.[29]

From a human perspective, the power of future tech seems at times almost indescribable. Viewed this way, it is understandable that people in our world will be so in awe of future technology that many of them will trade their faith in God for faith in human tech.[30] In fact, since tech is the amplification of human power, people who seek after new tech at all costs are, in effect, seeking after human power at all costs.[31] This is a critical truth. We need to take care that as we welcome new tech, we are not aiding in our further rebellion against God.

Since human power is limited, and only based on potentials, it will never be powerful enough to solve our problems and save our world. It will never make us holy.

The power of humans is what they can do through tech. The power of God is what God has done through people.

SPIT AND MUD

The words *Jesus* and *technology* occupy space in the same sentence rather uncomfortably. Because we tend to frame Jesus primarily in terms of what he said about God and life and the care he extended to people, including those on the margins, and the miracles that he did to demonstrate who he was, and his sacrifices on our behalf, we don't think often about his interaction with technology. Jesus never commented on tech, as far as we know. Yet Jesus used human technology—from shoes to boats to minted coins to paved roads. It was a part of his human activity the same as it is for us.

As a biblical scholar by trade, I'm interested in what the Bible says, but I'm also interested in what it leaves out. For example, contemporary Christians spend a great deal of time debating the morality of movies. Yet neither Paul nor Jesus spent any time on this—or if they did, the writers of the New Testament weren't inspired to include their thoughts. Now you may object: "But there were no movies in Jesus' and Paul's day!" But live plays were a popular pastime, especially in urban areas, and many of the plays of their day would be considered R-rated (or worse) by today's standards. Why did Jesus and Paul and Peter and James not weigh in on plays? Surely the theater of their day would have provided critical lessons by which they could have helped people better navigate culture.

Similarly, neither Jesus nor Paul nor the other New Testament writers weigh in on technology—even though they were surrounded by it. From loom-woven clothing to forged swords to quickset concrete, they lived in an advanced technological world compared to that of early humans. Why didn't biblical writers give guidance on technology?

Jesus himself even used technology to demonstrate his power. The Gospel of John records an event in which Jesus used a poultice as a practical step in a miraculous healing: "After saying this, [Jesus] spit on the ground, made some mud with the saliva, and put it on the man's eyes ... So the man went and washed, and came home seeing" (John 9:6-7).

Scholars have debated why Jesus would use a poultice, especially one made with spit and mud, and then make the man go wash.[32] As we saw with the examples of olive oil and soap that we discussed in earlier chapters, ancient people knew things worked, but they didn't always know why. (Modern scientists don't always know why things work, either.)

The Roman historian Tacitus, who wrote at the same time as John, records another story about the use of spit as salve.[33] In this story, a man with poor eyesight begs the emperor Vespasian to rub his eyes with his spit. Vespasian, not a fool, has his doctors examine the man. They report that the man cannot see well, but that some medical attention could help his condition. If Vespasian handles it correctly, there is no chance of a loss of honor for the emperor. So Vespasian applies spit to the man's eyes and the man starts to see better.[34]

Vespasian was a man who tried a common cure that he hoped had the potential to heal. Jesus was God incarnate who applied a common cure that he knew actually would heal— because God had already made it happen. Jesus even points this out when he says, "This happened so that the works of God might be displayed in him" (John 9:3).

Jesus didn't need the poultice to heal the man, but he made use of it because it meant something to the people witnessing it. God doesn't need antibiotics and computed tomography (CT or CAT) scans to heal people, but God makes use of them because they mean something to us.

Future technologies like intelligent robots will imbue humanity with an even greater sense of power than it has now. Our culture will tell us that our power is perfected in our greatness. It's not. Our power is perfected in our weakness (see 2 Corinthians 12:9).

SEVEN
TRANSCENDENCE NANOTECHNOLOGY AND BIOHACKERS

We've made a breakthrough with the nanotechnology. We can rebuild any material faster than before. Synthetic stem cells, tissue regeneration—the medical applications are now limitless. . . . They'll be scared at first, but once they see what the technology can do, I think that they will embrace it. And I think it will change their lives.

—DR. WILL CASTER, *TRANSCENDENCE*

Creepy is the only word that I could use to describe seeing Will alive again. Except that Will wasn't alive in the sense that most people mean it. No, Will Caster was not among the living; the polonium-laced bullet that took his life meant the end of a normal, physical existence for him. But Max Waters and Evelyn Caster, Will's wife, had accomplished the miraculous—transferring Will's mind and essence via a brain-computer interface into an AI that existed online. But seeing him "alive" again on the computer terminal was not a point of rejoicing; it did not bring me comfort. As Will's friend, I had been at his graveside; I had watched his body go into the ground. That was the Will Caster I knew. This vision on the screen wasn't Will . . . it was something else entirely.

The old Will Caster was a brilliant scientist whose work contributed to one field of science and technology in such a way that it might one day make the world a little better. The new Will Caster was a superbrilliant AI whose work contributed to many fields of science and technology in such a way that it would very soon make the world much better—that is, if our world were to give Will control to make it "better." Around him various groups fought for control over the technology; each believed their motives were better than the others' motives. Who was right? Was it better to lose a little control to have greater tech? Or was it better to have less tech—along with more sickness and suffering—but more control over our lives?

That, then, becomes the crux of the matter: How far do we trust technology? How willing are we to cede control to tech—switch on autopilot—over areas of our lives? Do we trust an autopilot in a metal tube with four jet engines to fly and land safely? Do we trust an autopilot in a surgery room to cut our bodies in the right place? Do we trust an autopilot in our bank account to pick the best investments for our family, our retirement, and our grandkids? Where, if anywhere, do we draw the line?

The movie *Transcendence*, written by Jack Paglen and directed by Wally Pfister, is in many ways a two-hour commercial for both limitless tech and transhumanism. It depicts a rapid increase in tech advancement that turns into the singularity through the creation of a super-intelligent AI. According to the movie, once someone triggers this event, it will become largely unstoppable.

And many believe that's a good thing, because its long term effect will be that future tech (such as nanotechnology) will remake our world into a paradise. *Transcendence* also tries to illustrate the ways various groups will feel and react to any possible singularity event. Scientists who are directly involved will applaud it; groups concerned about the ramifications of tech will oppose it; and the government will try to control it. Though the actual conflict over rapid tech will be more messy and complex than what *Transcendence* portrays, it is true that various groups will hold impassioned positions on how, when, and where we should deploy this kind of advanced technology.

I'm not worried about the singularity, but I am worried about how people will handle the singularity. Here's an example of my worry: Because the movie broaches the subjects of limitless tech and transhumanism, there is now a good bit of talk about the meaning and implications of the movie on the internet. It is quite shocking to read post after post from real people (presumably not trolls) who think that Will Caster's character was right to force other people to accept his technological advancements because they were "for the greater good." The many comments reveal that some of our population believes that we should give a scientist or even an AI carte blanche to "improve" our world without checks and balances.

But as I noted above, we live in a world where people more and more see tech as a god or king. Scientists and engineers, then, become the priests who mediate this new reality. This is that brave new world.

All these rapid changes will occur not just in the world that we can see but in the world we cannot. Tech is advancing on all levels, and it is poised to remake our world from the molecular level up.

SAMPLE TECH: NANOTECHNOLOGY

End-of-the-world scenarios often involve strange-sounding future tech. Of all the technologies we have explored, nanotechnology has an oversized share of apocalyptic possibilities ascribed to it. One of the most famous cataclysms involving nanotechnology is the so-called "grey goo" scenario. The idea behind this is that scientists will create nanobots (nano-sized robots) that use existing resources to self-replicate. In other words, nanobots would create new nanobots to make the work go more efficiently. This self-replication of nanobots would eventually get out of control (think of the same type of curve as the singularity is on), resulting in a nearly infinite number of nanobots transforming resources and spawning even more nanobots. The result would be that the nanobots would transform everything in our world into either more nanobots or their products, which would kill all life on the planet. Eventually everything in the known universe would become one big, grey ball of goo. Though this is a favorite catastrophe among sci-fi writers, there is little evidence that this could occur. The scientist who lit the fuse of speculation has since explained why it cannot happen in actuality.[1]

In fact, nanotechnology is a near-future tech that could help revolutionize every area of our world for the better. One way that nanotech will do this is by making everything that we do much more efficient than the way we do everything now. For example, right now the primary way we remove harmful bacteria from an ill person is to use a mechanical process to strain the blood. As a result of this pint-by-pint approach to straining, the process is difficult for the patient and inefficient at catching bacteria. However, a nanotech solution creates a highly efficient straining system for harmful bacteria that allows doctors to clean the blood on the nano level.[2]

A similar example occurs with the production of clean water in dry or polluted areas of the Earth. Right now, the only options available are to try to clean polluted water, desalinize ocean water, or pray for rain. The first two require significant amounts of energy and large-scale technologies; the last, an act of God. In contrast, a recent tech invention uses a nanonet to catch water that exists in the air. It only requires a small device that is cheap to manufacture. Best of all, because the nanonet actually catches the water in a physical process, no energy is required.[3]

So what is nanotechnology? It is technology that works on the nano level. *Nano* is the scientific prefix for one billionth, so a nanometer is one billionth of a meter, a nanoliter is one billionth of a liter, and so on. Nanotechnology is technology that works with materials measured in nanometers. A nanometer is a super tiny length—so tiny it is impossible to imagine. These materials that are in the nano range can be as small as an atom or as large as a molecule. This size range is smaller than a virus, and significantly smaller than a bacterium.[4]

This doesn't completely explain the importance of nanotechnology, however. The reason nanotechnology is so powerful is *not* because of its tiny size. The reason nanotechnology is so powerful is that when materials get to a certain minimum size, they start to act differently than they do when they are at larger *or* smaller sizes, such as the size that we can see with the naked eye.[5] Using the example above, a net woven from materials we find present in our world cannot pull water out of the sky, but a net can do so when it is woven from particles so small they behave differently than their regular-sized counterparts. Humans are skilled at building tech out of plastic, wood, concrete, and steel, as these are some of the best materials we know. We are not likely to discover better materials than these in the world we can see. But there is a whole world of new materials waiting to be discovered by manipulating molecules on the nano level. The plastic, wood, concrete, and steel of the twenty-second century are all yet to be discovered and replicated in a nanolab.

Nanotechnology is a far more efficient approach to doing work because it works like we do, not like we think we do. Let me explain. Our bodies, created by God and adapted to the physical planet on which we live, accomplish a great deal of work we take for granted, because the work being done is on levels far too small for us to see. From capillaries to DNA, our bodies work on a tiny level even as we go about our day, doing tasks on an everyday level. Tech that allows us to work on a tiny level (in this case, a nano level) is, in some sense, more "natural" than the way we work today (on the macro level).[6]

Nanotechnology will really begin to change the world when it begins to impact other future tech. From artificial intelligence to gene editing to smart materials to the Internet of Things, nanotechnology will redefine all of these technologies. For example, once we have figured out how to transfer rudimentary information about a person to a computer via a brain-computer interface, nanotechnology will supercharge that interface and bring a far sharper transfer than could be realized through everyday means.[7] Nanotechnology is recognized as a possible sign that the singularity is near. Nanotech will allow us to do things that we never thought possible. We will have the tools to create and recreate almost anything we can imagine.

At first glance, unlike most of the other sample technologies we have explored, nanotech doesn't seem to have an obvious downside. This tech is merely existing materials redesigned, from the nano up. Surprisingly, though, studies suggest that significant percentages of Westerners—especially people in the United States—oppose nanotechnology.[8] Is it because we have only scratched the surface of new materials and new technologies that will come from the nanotech revolution? Or is it because nanotechnology will supercharge all other future tech? What is happening?

PLAYING GOD?

With the ability to create, change, and destroy on the nano level, humanity will possess an unprecedented power to remake our world. As the 3D printer is to the first coal-fired industrial plant, so too is nanotechnology to modern building materials. This power will usher in a new sense of omnipotence; seemingly anything will now be possible. Coupled with technology such as gene editing, nanotechnology will empower us to make alterations to our world, our species, and ourselves.

The charge that some will level against this new tech is that we are "playing God." This is an idea that culture will trumpet in order to create a wedge between science and faith.[9] Don't believe it. No human being has the power to play God. Yes, it's true, humans can try to usurp God's authority, they can use their power to do evil instead of good, and generally speaking, humans can make a mess of things.[10] Yet God created people to think, to explore, to wonder, and to create. When we use modern tech such as eyeglasses to see better, we are not playing

God; we are being faithful to the good abilities granted to us by our Creator. When we use future tech such as nanotechnology to see in the infrared and ultraviolet spectrums, we are not playing God; we are being faithful to the good abilities given to us by our Creator. In the former, to heal; in the latter, to create.

"Aren't these two examples apples and oranges?" some may wonder. "One corrects a damaged part of the body, and the other is an enhancement that goes beyond what we consider to be human."[11] This is an argument that some philosophers and theologians make—that tech can be used to cure but should not be used to enhance.[12] One of the arguments is that enhancing our bodies through nanotechnology or gene editing is a fundamentally selfish act.

The problem with these academic arguments is that they take place in a theoretical world that doesn't look much like our real world. In the real world, it is hard to avoid selfish acts, for good and bad reasons. In the morning, we get up, we shower, we brush our teeth, we comb our hair. That's an hour wasted on vanity. Doesn't working out make us look and feel our best; is that, too, a selfish act? Though we may strive for it, there is no way that humans can be completely altruistic in all they do, every second of the day. It's just not possible.

Is bioenhancement morally wrong? Let's consider plastic surgery as an example: plastic surgery is the tech, and we choose to use it or not based on a wide variety of reasons and motivations. We can use it well, and we can use it poorly, like any tool. It is easy for us to envision noble reasons for plastic surgery (such as for burn victims), and it is easy for us to envision ignoble reasons for plastic surgery (such as the growing number of unusual forms of cosmetic nips, tucks, and implants). This is simply because human enhancement is not, in and of itself, wrong.[13] This doesn't mean that the motivations for enhancement are always pure, or that it won't cause us moral and spiritual issues.

I don't want to cherry-pick the argument, so let's consider another example of bioenhancement that exists today: performance-enhancing drugs. Are performance-enhancing drugs morally wrong? In our world today, it's hard to think of a scenario in which these drugs would be considered morally acceptable. But again, these drugs are technologies that we use for a wide variety of reasons and motivations. Currently, most of these drugs are either experimental or unhealthy, are obtained through less than legal means, and are used to break rules or laws (usually to cheat at sports). These factors shade the use of the tech. Here we have a tech for which the motivations for enhancement are poor, which is why it causes moral, spiritual, and legal issues.

Truth time: I am on a performance-enhancing drug right now, as I write this. The drug is called caffeine, and the beverage manufacturer added it to the soda I just finished (presumably for taste, but, c'mon!). It's selfish of me, because I could just drink water instead of indulging myself in this unhealthy bioenhancement. Whether my use of tech this way is morally wrong, I will let you, the reader, be the judge.

As a professor, I constantly grade students' papers in which they use the passive voice. Something about the passive makes it sound more studied, or lofty. But writing in the passive "hides the subject"—a phrase I am eternally writing on student papers. The problem with "playing God" is that that statement also hides the subject. Who, exactly, is playing God? If someone uses nanotechnology to enhance their body, is the enhancer playing God? Or the doctor who performs the procedure? Are we back to giving tech agency, such that it is the tech that is playing God?

We again come to the conclusion that it is not the tech itself that is the problem; it is what people do with tech that can be the problem. Each participant will have different roles and agendas. If we "solve" the people, we solve tech. Otherwise, we are stuck in a circle.

SACRIFICES TO THE NEWEST MASTER OF THE UNIVERSE

In college, I majored in chemistry. I think I chose that as my major because it was a scientific discipline that allowed me to be involved in experimentation, not just sit around and discuss ideas. It seemed tangible and real. My favorite courses were in instrumental analysis and physical chemistry (I hated organic chemistry; many people seem to quit chemistry because of organic, which is a pity).

When I went to graduate school right after college, I needed a job, and doing odd jobs around campus, like many other students, didn't seem the best way to pay the bills. After sending my résumé out, I was hired as a chemist, and I worked in a lab in which I managed robotic-controlled gas chromatographs/ mass spectrometers (GC/MSs). Though I am thankful for that experience, the job probably sounds cooler than it was. Much of my job entailed keeping up with the robot. As the GC/MS analyzed samples, my primary focus was to make sure the analyses were correct and that we were receiving good data. Since I worked in a commercial—not research—lab, I also had to keep the GC/MS robot stocked with new samples. I was constantly "feeding the machine." But the machine never got full; it always wanted more.

The more tech grows, and the more it plays a central focus in our lives, the more it will demand greater and greater sacrifices from us. This is the reason why the line between healing people and enhancing people is blurry.[14] The more we are able to heal diseases, the smaller the "disease" becomes. In the past, diseases were tuberculosis and cholera, but now diseases are coronary artery disease and Alzheimer's—diseases that we didn't even know about until the twentieth century. In ages past, people didn't understand Alzheimer's to be a disease—they just thought it meant getting old. It would not be incorrect to say that from a nineteenth-century perspective, healing a person of Alzheimer's would be a life-extending enhancement.

I hope one day soon we discover a cure for Alzheimer's. Most of my paternal relatives died due to Alzheimer's; that disease is in my genes, too. So I am all in on that enhancement. Yet the more tech improves our lives, the more we will feel obligated to let it improve our lives. And the more we will want it to improve our lives. We will keep "feeding the machine" of self-improvement. As soon as my neighbor was cured of his nearsightedness, I had to get myself some glasses. As soon as my neighbor enhances herself with infrared or ultraviolet vision, will I have to have that type of vision, too?

The curious thing about the twenty-first century is that some people are not waiting for the future; they are getting the bioenhancement party started right now. Already in our world there are people known as biohackers.[15] This word comes from the combination of *bio-* and *hacker*. When personal computers first became available, they were expensive; when they dropped in price, many people bought them, which gave freedom to people to do anything they wanted, including unauthorized things (hacking). Because biological and medical equipment is becoming less costly and easier to access, it is giving people the freedom to do anything they want, including "unauthorized" things. Pop culture uses biohacking to mean anything from radical body modifications (think the guy with the synthetic horns implanted on his head) to "playing God" with E. coli bacteria on their kitchen sink with a CRISPR-Cas9.[16] Here I don't use *biohacking* to mean extreme tattoos, fad diets, or gizmos ordered from late night infomercials. Instead, I intend the word *biohack* to be used in a narrower sense: experimental procedures that a person tries out on their own body in the hopes of jump-starting their personal transhuman evolution.[17] Examples include the growing number of Swedes who are inserting microchips in their bodies;[18] or "grinders," extreme biohackers, who are working toward body modifications and genetic editing.[19] This takes "feeding the machine" to a whole new level.

CLIMBING UP TO GOD

Once we have started hacking our way toward immortality, we are poised to do what every other generation of human being has hoped to do: unseat God from the place of authority in our universe. We will have the tools, the hubris, the will. What is it that makes people do anything and everything, direct or indirect, in their quest to be equal to God?

We remember the apostle Paul's famous admonition: "Let each of you look not only to his own interests, but also to the interests of others. Have this mind among yourselves, which is yours in Christ Jesus, who, though he was in the form of God, did not count equality with God a thing to be grasped" (Philippians 2:4-6 ESV). Paraphrased, Paul says we are not to be selfish only, but to care for others, because this is what Jesus did; even though he was God himself, he didn't try to climb to heaven but spent his time ministering to others.

Does humanity keep trying to climb up to God because we are full of arrogance in our rebellion? Or does being made in the image of God compel humanity to seek out divine properties—an unrequited attempt at theosis made through self-focus and self-evolution?[20] Either way, as humanity drives forward progress, we need to evaluate where that forward progress will take us. Nanotechnology will give us the ability to rebuild the world from the ground up. But what kind of world should we build? Humanism and transhumanism are both isms founded on the idea that we can escape the limitations of this world and be like God.[21] Our Western culture has been swept up in these isms for centuries; the future promises more of the same, just more powerful currents than before sweeping humanity along. And we can't blame it on the tech. Whatever we do, the tech didn't make us do it.

Not only is it impossible for humans to grasp equality with God, but the attempt can be a dangerous enterprise. Just as the slopes of Mount Everest are littered with the detritus of previous attempts, so too are the slopes of heaven littered with the isms of humanity and their many failed attempts.[22] We don't want to be in that group.

My father was not a transhumanist—and by that, I mean I don't think he would have recognized the word. Nor was he interested in philosophy. He just loved, and believed in, science.[23] Like Ben Franklin and Ray Kurzweil, he believed that science and technology were on the cusp of solving most major medical issues. He believed that if he could just live a few more years, science would have answers for most things, from the common cold to Alzheimer's. He died believing that technology could soon save him; he believed it was almost there. But in the end, tech didn't save him, and it never would have, because tech is the savior of no human. I, too, love science, and I am confident that we will one day have tech solutions to both the common cold and Alzheimer's. But save the world, it cannot do. And tech will not save me or you.

We need to be careful about what we put our faith in, even in small ways. One of the most solvent critiques of transhumanism is not its promotion of technology; rather, it is the false hopes that culture often uses tech to promote.[24] "Believe in tech and one day soon you may live forever!" is the carnival-barker cry of a segment of our media. If we drill down into this, we find that it is not faith in tech that is the problem; it is the lack of faith in the Creator's presence in, and plan for, our world. This lack of faith is not evidenced in the technology itself (at least, not usually); it is hidden in the promotion and packaging and reception of the tech in our world.[25] It is based on a half-truth. In our mixed-up, muddled-up, shook-up world, nothing sells like half-truths.[26]

The irony is this: we are running headlong toward technologies that will be superior to humanity, all because humanity cannot admit or accept the God who already is superior to us. We'll build this god in our image, and it will make us feel even better about ourselves than we already do. But it will be built on the half-truth of who we are.

Remember when Jesus said, "Do not be afraid of those who kill the body but cannot kill the soul" (Matthew 10:28)? Without diminishing Jesus' original point, allow me to paraphrase this for our future world of limitless tech: "Don't be afraid of those who want to enhance your body but cannot enhance your soul."

IMPECCABLE

We humans think we are most excellent, don't we? Secretly, many of us believe we are, right? Our social media presence is proof positive.

Way back in the 1980s, there was a little-known movie about two dudes trying to graduate from high school. It was a bogus situation, because they were on the verge of failing their history class. These two dudes have to graduate from high school because the future depends on it—if they stay on track, one day their music will bring utopia to the planet, maybe even the entire universe. To make sure they graduate, a future dude comes to them and lets them travel back in time to complete their history report so that they can graduate. The world they will create? Near perfect. As the future dude, Rufus, says, "The air is clean, the water's clean, even the dirt, it's clean. Bowling averages are way up, mini-golf scores are way down. And we have more excellent water slides than any other planet we communicate with."[27] It truly sounds almost perfect.

Who knew Bill and Ted were transhumanists? Bill and Ted use future tech to evolve to the next level of musicianship, and their music encourages all of humanity to evolve to the next stage. We'll no longer be *Homo sapiens*; not exactly *Homo deus*, I suppose, but certainly *Homo bodacious*. In doing so, the world approaches perfection: tech has transformed our planet, and because of it, now people have plenty of time to perfect their mini-golf scores.

Our sense of our own excellence is a temptation that is often too great to overcome. And future tech will encourage that sense to grow in our lives. The better life becomes, the more we are at risk of not recognizing our own selfish, broken, hurting, and hurtful condition. And the better life becomes, the more we are at risk of not recognizing the hurting conditions of the people around us.

There is one aspect of who God is that creates a great deal of friction between God and humanity. That aspect is God's impeccable nature. When we describe God as impeccable, it means we are saying that God is not able to sin. But that's in the most basic sense; there is a little more to it than that. God is not able to sin, but it is not because God is morally unable; it is because God's nature is perfect and not lacking anything in and of itself. God is holy, because he is integral, complete, sufficient; he is the end all and be all of . . . everything. In fact, God even tells us this, recorded in Scripture when Moses asks what God's name is. How does God respond? God says that we can tell people that his name is "I am who I am" (see Exodus 3:14). God is not dependent on anything; thus there is no weakness or limitation in him. God is all there is. God is perfect.

Human beings, however, are decidedly not perfect. When we say it this way, it's easy to get most people to agree that human beings have weaknesses, are broken, and make mistakes. Sometimes that truth gets lost when we think about all the marvels of the future. Sure, we are not perfect, the thinking goes; but maybe future generations will be closer to perfection than we are. Even in the last century, the rapid increases in food production, medicine, and overall living conditions make it seem as if we are slowly but surely moving toward a period in which we won't have major needs. Unfortunately, no matter the power of tech, humanity will never be able to overcome its sinfulness through human means. This is because our brokenness runs much deeper than our physical bodies. It strikes us to our very souls.

This debate is actually not new. Way, way back in the early fifth century, for example, the idea that some people could achieve perfection in this life, by the power of their own will, became popular in some circles. The early church father Jerome wrote against this idea to help people realize that accepting their limitations was essential to living well in our world: "This is true wisdom in man: to know that he is imperfect . . . [Those] who wish to be perfect, according to the measure of human frailty, be of this mind, that we have not yet obtained [perfection]; that we have not yet laid hold of it; that we have not yet been made perfect. . . . not only are men not perfect, in comparison with the divine majesty, but not even in comparison with angels and other men who have reached the heights of virtues."[28]

Jerome's words are as valid today as when he wrote them sixteen hundred years ago. True wisdom starts by recognizing our weaknesses and our imperfections. Our lives are much frailer than we would like to admit.

There is a huge danger with the coming future tech that is actually far riskier than that depicted in dystopian sci-fi movies from Hollywood. In those depictions, the danger is that the singularity will result in good tech being put to evil use. A far greater threat to humanity is that the singularity will result in good tech being put to good use. Yes, you read that right; with good tech being put to good use, it will be easy for our descendants to believe that they don't really have problems, that they are closing in on perfection. They will clean the outside of the cup—through gene editing, nanotechnology, and cybernetics—while the inside of the cup will remain dirty (see Matthew 23:25-28). The more wonderful our external lives look, the more miserable our internal lives may prove to be.

Just take a look at your Facebook or Instagram feeds—they are full of people whose bowling averages are way up and mini-golf scores are way down. Not a hint of imperfection anywhere to be found.

SEAMLESS TUNIC

When we read the Bible, we are conditioned to read it through a religious lens. This means that we are susceptible to missing important details. It's not that reading the Bible religiously is wrong; it's that reading it through any narrow lens unwisely limits our understanding. For example, many readers of the Bible are not prepared to read the Bible as literature, so they don't stop to think about why a writer of a text says things a certain way.

One of the details of the biblical text that we miss is technology. Because the Bible doesn't directly address technology ("Thou shalt not put thy data on a cloud"), we tend not to think about it much when we read Scripture. Yet the Bible is full of technology. For example:

- Some human forebears in the earliest genealogies were known by their lifestyles (lived in tents) and technology, including tools made of bronze and iron (see Genesis 4:20-22).
- Rahab hid the Hebrew spies on her roof among the raw materials meant for her horizontal weaving loom (see Joshua 2:6).[29]
- The crew of Paul's ship use sounding leads as an early form of sonar (see Acts 27:28).
- A well-engineered aqueduct brought the cold water of Laodicea in from the mountains and siphoned it into a water tower (see Revelation 3:15).

There are far too many more to list here.

Beyond these simple examples, God commanded humans to build at least two tech marvels to exact specifications: the ark (see Genesis 6:14–16) and the tabernacle (see Exodus 25:9–27:19). The majestic beauty of these tech innovations was more impressive to the people of that day than the latest iteration of the iPhone is to us. If God commanded people to engage in tech in the past—out of obedience, for the glory of God—is it any wonder people still want to engage in tech today?

Why is the Bible full of technology and yet lacking specific guidance and direction about it? Is it possible that our debate about tech is more of a red herring than we would believe? Is it possible that tech doesn't matter much to God?

There is one technology that is close to God's own heart—literally. We know that in Jesus' time on Earth, he wore a tunic that was without seams (see John 19:23-24). Bible readers and scholars have discussed and extrapolated the meaning (and secret meanings) of the mention of this tunic for two thousand years. My training leads me to believe that the primary reason John mentions the tunic is because he liked to include little eyewitness details that give the reader a feeling of veracity as they read, and to explain how these details demonstrate Jesus' fulfillment of the Hebrew Scriptures. Not anything more than that.

But let's ponder this interesting detail a bit further. It's possible that, because it was seamless, it was woven by hand. My maternal grandmother used to crochet wonderful afghans that her great-grandchildren still use. To make a seamless tunic that way would require a bit of tech and a bit of human industry. However, there is another equally possible scenario: that Jesus' tunic was created on a "modern" vertical loom. At some point in antiquity, someone invented a vertical loom to replace the less efficient horizontal loom. In fact, the white garments mentioned in Revelation are a reference to the seamless, shiny black wool garments made on high-tech looms in Laodicea (see Revelation 3:18).[30]

Whether you want to envision Jesus wearing a homemade, hand-woven seamless tunic, or a high-tech, fine wool seamless tunic, I'll leave that to you. One thing we can say for certain: As Jesus goes to the cross, he is adorned with human technology—and there he is executed with human technology. Both the tunic and the cross are the results of human tech. One clothed our Savior, and one was the means by which he was killed. Both were put to use by human hands.

EIGHT

SELF/LESS
CYBERNETICS AND THE
GLORY OF TECH

Well, all of our clients are wealthy, but that's not how they're chosen. No, we cater to the great, the visionaries, whose loss would be a blow to all of us. Simply put, we offer humanity's greatest minds more time to fulfill their potential. If you think about it, your homes, your yacht, your jet . . . all custom-built by the world's finest craftsmen. And so will your new body be as well. Genetically engineered for perfection. Harvested to maturity so looks, athleticism, every detail of your new anatomy will be designed to offer you the very best of the human experience.

—ALBRIGHT / PROFESSOR FRANCIS JENSEN, *SELF/LESS*

W hen Damian Hale entered his new body, Damian ended and Edward Kidner began. In his old life, Damian was an aging and ailing billionaire real estate developer from New York City. But in his new life, Edward Kidner is a rejuvenated young man at the peak of physical fitness, with the muscle memory of a trained soldier to boot. If you had met Damian in his old life and Edward in his new life, you would notice that Edward doesn't seem to act much like Damian did. The smugness is gone. But the drive to win at all costs is close—or close enough. The new body that Damian has, and his new identity as Edward, begs the question: who is this person now—Damian or Edward?

Damian Hale is one of the world's elite; there is no success he hasn't tasted and no excess he hasn't sought. Yet the one thing he cannot conquer is his own mortality. Hale is dying, and for the first time in his life, he is powerless to do something about it. On the tip from a friend, Hale learns about Phoenix Biogenic, a secretive company that Damian visits in hope of finding a cure. There, one of the tech company's lead scientists named Albright introduces Damian to the idea of "shedding": the transfer of a dying person's mind into a genetically engineered body. This tech allows a person to shed their old body for a new one, thereby extending life indefinitely. The future Albright presents to Damian is one in which the elite can be reborn into new bodies, giving them a second chance, over and over again. And why not? These are people who have succeeded at the game of life—don't they deserve it?

This is the future of *Self/less*, from the film by Tarsem Singh, based on the screenplay by Alex and David Pastor. Though it seems to be set in a time period much like tomorrow, in this world, tech has progressed to the point that a person can skip over medical treatments and cybernetic repairs and simply shed their old bodies for new ones. The villain of *Self/less* is Francis Jensen, who is overtly revealed to be an evil transhumanist. The contrast between *Transcendence* and *Self/less* is fascinating. In both movies, a rogue scientist achieves a singularity or near-singularity event, but in the former the audience is meant to feel sympathetic toward the scientist; in the latter, the audience is mean to feel disdain. Both films present radical life extension as unpalatable even though most people seem to want to live long, healthy lives.

As I was watching *Self/less* with my wife, she pointed out something that only a people person might notice: both characters mouth their moral viewpoints with full self assurance. Neither stops to wonder if they should check their perspectives with others. As I noted above, *Transcendence* worked in much the same way, with each side convinced of their own moral superiority.

Maybe this suggests the deeper meaning of these movies. Whether any particular tech is good or bad is somewhat beside the point. The more important question is whether humans are so self-focused that they are unwilling to consult with others on the wisdom of its use. Maybe the problem isn't tech. Maybe the problem never was tech. Maybe the problem is us.

As we peer deeper into the future, the murkier it gets as far as where tech will go. One thing we can say with certainty: The more tech changes, the more people will stay the same— on the inside, at least.

Yet while none of us can predict the future of tech, it is safe to say that there is a certain triumph of tech in the making. This will prove to be true whether we like it or not, and whether we are prepared for it or not. In point of fact, as cybernetics begins to unfold, this triumph is already occurring around us. We are the proverbial frog in the pot as tech slowly heats up around us—we'll never jump out of it.[1] Will cybernetics finally push humanity over the edge? Will we have more power and fewer freedoms? Will we have more pleasure but less character? Will we have greater heavens as well as greater hells? Will the human isms that accompany tech be supportive of, or antagonistic to, faith?

SAMPLE TECH: CYBERNETICS

Of all the different kinds of great sci-fi supervillains, cyborgs are the greatest. From the Borg to Daleks to Cylons, from Darth Vader to the T-800 Terminator, cyborgs inhabit a special place in our imaginations when it comes to future tech. Compared to robots (such as Decepticons), AIs (such as Agent Smith), clones (such as Stormtroopers), aliens (such as Thanos), or just plain evil humans (such as the Joker), cyborgs wield an undue influence. They represent the bridge between the organic and the inorganic, the human and the alien, the human and the machine. Somehow, this is more frightening to more people than other kinds of sci-fi villains. Why do cyborgs seem so unnatural? What does a cybernetic age portend for humanity? And for faith?

Cyborg is short for a "cybernetic organism."[2] In pop culture, *cybernetics* is any type of technology that allows robot parts to help, improve, or supplant our natural, biological form. In this sense of the word, future people with metal limbs and plastic organs could be considered cyborgs. Even in our world today, you could say that "cyborgs" are all around us: people with pacemakers, cochlear implants, insulin pumps, and dental implants are examples of cybernetic humans. That four-foot-ten grandma with a titanium hip joint? Yep, technically, she's a cyborg. Of course, there is much more to being a cyborg in its fullest sense than just adding a prosthesis or experimental implants.[3] Cybernetics is actually a broader field of study than depicted by pop culture and sci-fi writers.

To put it in perspective, a metal body part is to cybernetics as a gear is to industrialization. It's a part of a whole area, but only a small and very early part. Generally defined, cybernetics is any tech that provides control over both organic and inorganic material.[4] In other words, cybernetics speaks to communication and information as much as it does to bits and chips.

Of all the technologies I have covered in this book, cybernetics is the one that will change who we are as people more than any other. This is because cybernetics is not limited to just metal parts; cybernetics requires us to rethink how our old "parts" work with our new parts. It requires us to communicate with, and gain information from, mechanical and computerized components that become one with our bodies. Cyborgs can no longer think merely as people; they must think as machines, too. They will straddle the gap between the organic and inorganic, and they will flatten our worlds completely.[5] More than anything else, cybernetics will fundamentally change our bodies, minds, and even our souls. Cybernetics will change who we are, and what it means to be human.

Already we begin to see implications. For example, who "controls" new cybernetic parts? In the past, mechanical implants were mostly "dumb," so there was little debate. But as mechanical parts move toward becoming smart mechanical parts, some cyborgs (in the sense we mean it today) are fighting to have control over the parts of their bodies (such as control over their own pacemakers), not simply leaving it to the parts' manufacturers. This includes releasing the means to personally control their own body parts, perhaps against the recommendations of doctors and makers.[6]

And when people can't get control? They turn to hacking—in this case, hacking themselves. This is what happened when one color-blind biohacker added a color-sensing antenna to his brain. Using his cybernetic antenna, he is now able to see color "vibrations," including those within the infrared and ultraviolet spectrum.[7] What will be next?

It's hard to say what will happen to us, and what will happen to our world, once we start plugging advanced hardware into our biologically designed wetware. If, for example, some people start to see color vibrations outside of the visible light spectrum, it will start to alter their perception of the world, and how they think, and what they think with these new parts. As each tech we surveyed comes online, it will create profound ripples across all other techs. The farther into the future we go, the harder it is to see. And the more romantic science becomes in our present-day minds.

If nanotechnology is a sign that the singularity is imminent, the first "full" cyborg will be the sign that we have crossed the threshold to something posthuman.[8] What is a "full" cyborg, in comparison to the very limited cyborgs we know of today? That's hard to even say—we won't know it until we see it. We do know it will be a human with biological, mechanical, and AI features all working together resulting in a power heretofore unseen in humanity (maybe the ability to interface their mind with a computer or the ability to live an exceptionally long life). These posthuman people may very well adopt the mantra "Be strong in technology and in its mighty power. Put on the full metal of your cybernetic humanity, so that you can take your place at the head of this world" (cf. Ephesians 6:10-11). If all this feels a bit weird, that's your humanity calling you back to a world of earlier tech.

THE TRIUMPH OF TECH

I grew up in a time when playing videogames mostly meant having a quarter in your pocket. I do still remember the first time I laid eyes on an Atari 2600; it was the most amazing thing I had ever seen. TV media had subjected me to relentless advertising about it. But to hold one of those square, black controllers in my hand after a Cub Scout meeting at a friend's house? It was world-changing. My parents were not quick to purchase those kinds of things, and they doled out quarters too infrequently for my taste. I ended up playing videogames as much as I could with a few quarters here and there, until high school when I could get myself to the houses of friends who had the newest home videogame systems.

The only videogame I ever really played—and was addicted to—after high school was Sid Meier's *Civilization* (every iteration). The point of *Civilization* is to start in the ancient world, develop a historical civilization through time, and, eventually, rule the world before you reach the space age.[9] There's nothing like advancing through the tech trees to surpass your enemies—they move into attack formation with a horde of spearmen while you sit, unconcerned, with cities defended by musket men. Here's the best part: If you close in on the space age without defeating your enemies, at some point the tech advancements you receive just become nameless, undefined "future tech."

How the triumph of tech plays out in our world is still very much to be determined. For the cyborgs of our future world, the goal is utopia, but getting there will prove to be as elusive as getting to a utopia has always been. This is because the concept of utopia means different things to different people. Most everyone can agree that a clean planet where no one goes hungry, everyone is sheltered, disease is eradicated, and all are living at peace is a utopia worth working toward. We're actually much closer to these goals than we ever have been at any point in history past.

But before anyone thinks this is a "We are the World" moment, it's not. The problem is that we may only get to that beautiful place by a very, very messy road. It's a road littered with enhancements for the ultrawealthy; biohackers working outside the system; degradation of the value of human life; increases in all types of addictions, syndromes, and disorders; and a greater hubris in humanity, culture, and technology.[10]

If you read the stories that transhumanists promote, it is easy to hear their humanist underpinnings. If you listen even more closely, because these two isms originate in the Western tradition, you can hear the faint but clear sound of Christian theology within. Christians know that one day God is going to wrap up our broken world. We know that someday God will make the people who love God new again, in perfect bodies, and they will live forever in a land that flows with milk and honey. We may disagree about the specifics of how it will happen, but we have confidence in the stirring vision painted by the writer of Revelation, who assures us that "'He will wipe every tear from their eyes. There will be no more death' or mourning or crying or pain, for the old order of things has passed away" (Revelation 21:4).

Transhumanists and likeminded tech enthusiasts believe, in a peculiarly similar way, that one day technology will give humanity the power to wrap up our previous dark ages. They trust that tech will make the people who use it new again—people who will live very long lives in perfect bodies in a land that is unpolluted and at balance with itself. In Christian theology, the way to get to paradise is for a great high priest to mediate our way; in transhumanism, the way to get to paradise is for the world's priests (scientists and producers of tech) to mediate our way.[11]

From the world's perspective, I suspect most of the tech that comes our way will be sold to us as a part of the greater good—a way to jump-start our progress towards our own utopia. And as I have said, in many ways I look forward to the vision of that great future. I wish I could peer ahead and see the good that humanity will have achieved by the twenty-second century. But it's probably just as well that I can't, as I don't want to think about the horrors that also lie ahead. Tech may triumph, but it is not clear that good will—at least until God decides to intervene with his own singularity.

It's not easy to see over our own event horizon. To us, tech feels like it took off in maybe the 80s, maybe the 90s, depending on our age. Maybe we can imagine tech in the twentieth century, but any time before that, it becomes very, very difficult. It is impossible to understand what it was like to live a thousand years ago. Those ancestors of ours were human; they thought and felt like us. Yet if one of us moderns was placed for even a day into their lives, the sheer difficulty it would entail for us would be insurmountable—all due to our reliance on technology. Most of this is technology that we take for granted because it existed before we were born and is simply part of the background of the world in which we live.

This is bigger than just us, right now. Humanity's work is moving in a direction that has been building since the dawn of time. And I mean that literally; the Bible presents God as uncreated, but our world, time, and space are created (see John 1:1, Genesis 1:1-5). In the Garden of Eden, that direction we as humans were moving in went from a straight line to a zigzag, which has cast us as namers, creators, and producers into the fury of a wounded world. From humanity's point of view, writes architect and urban visionary William J. Mitchell:

> We are at the endgame of a process that began when our distant ancestors started to clothe themselves with second skins stripped from other creatures, to extend and harden their hands with simple tools and weapons, and to record information by scratching marks on surfaces. It picked up speed when our more recent forebears began to wire up telegraph, telephone, and packet-switching networks, to place calls, to log in, and to download dematerialized information to wireless portable devices. . . . It is not that we have become posthuman in the wireless network era; since Neanderthal early-adopters first picked up sticks and stones, we have never been human.[12]

From the moment humans left the Garden, tech has been humanity's constant companion. In fact, technology is an indirect result of God's curse on humanity. God made it clear that because of Adam's rebellion against God, his descendants would now have a difficult time living in this world (see Genesis 3:14-19). Since the world would no longer cooperate with Adam, he would need tools to make the world cooperate.

Maybe tech was unavoidable. Maybe when God put humanity out of the Garden, to master the world, humanity turned to tech instead of to God. Maybe the singularity is not actually the triumph of tech; maybe the triumph of tech came the first time Adam put his hand to the plow instead of his face toward God. Maybe tech has already won and all we do now is but a footnote to that established truth.

IN SEARCH OF GLORY

No one embraces death. Some may accept it, some may pursue it out of hurt or fear, some fight against it, some promote it, but no one embraces it. In many ways, death is the defining characteristic of what it means to be human. Every decision we make, every action we take, is predicated on the belief that we only have a limited time in this life. We try to preserve life at all costs. It is why the fountain of youth, were it to exist, would be considered the greatest treasure a person could find.[13]

The fountain of youth is exactly the end goal of technology empowered by transhumanist thought.[14] This is both an echo of Christian theology as well as a guttural reaction of physical bodies in a broken world. In fact, part of what it means to be human is to desire immortality.[15] While there is general agreement that technology will continue to extend lives, one of the great debates in science right now is whether technology can accomplish radical life extension. Life extension refers to helping people live longer, and in a more meaningful way, into their early hundreds. Radical life extension refers to helping people live vibrant lives for hundreds of years, if not longer. There is a qualitative difference, of course, between the transhumanist radical life-extension version of living forever and the Christian eternal life version of living forever. One understands living forever as improving ourselves here on Earth; the other understands living forever as resurrected life dwelling with God.

Are life extension—especially radical life extension—and eternal life competing ideas? Do we have to choose one or the other?

I don't believe so. Compared to the lives of our recent ancestors, our lives are already extended, and radically so. My life expectancy is almost double what the life expectancy of my ancestors was just ten generations ago.[16] Is that extension of life incompatible with the Christian view of eternal life? No. So if in the next twenty or forty years medical science uses gene therapy, cybernetics, nanoelectronics, and more to eliminate all major forms of disease and pushes my children's life expectancy to double that of my parents, will that be incompatible with the Christian view of eternal life? No. Regardless of how many times we extend human life, radically even, it is not the same—or even comparable—to our resurrection and dwelling with God.

Personally, I welcome life extension. I worry, though, that it will be applied unevenly; that it will become available primarily to the wealthy or the elite.[17] Still, I don't believe the naysayers who suggest it will ruin our economy or disprove our faith. Just as doubling the life expectancy we currently live with didn't destroy the world, neither will any future doubling of life expectancy. In fact, after it happens, it will just seem normal, as tech always feels once a generation has grown up with it.

Does that mean I believe that radical life extension is possible? Well, that's another issue; just because I hope for an improved world doesn't mean it will happen. In order for radical life extension to occur, not one but two profound changes in technology must happen. We would need to cure and heal many things we cannot currently cure and heal, and we would need to rejuvenate older bodies to a degree that we cannot rejuvenate them now. There is evidence that all of this is coming, but how soon and in what way, we simply do not know. My kids may very well expect to live to their early hundreds or beyond, but I do not. Bottom line: If we love life, if we are in favor of life in all its shades of meaning, then it is consistent for us to be in favor of extending life in every reasonable way.[18] From a glass half-full view, the longer people live, the more chances they get to hear the good news of God's redeeming love.

Every upside has a downside, and there is a major downside to the pursuit of radical life extension. Let me say it again—while life extension may be good, and even radical life extension may be good, the pursuit of it may be bad. We come back to human motivation and reasoning. Should humanity pursue life extension because we want to ease suffering and pain? We can applaud this pursuit. Should humanity pursue radical life extension because we want to avoid facing God? If that's the motivation, we see the problem there. In reality, the pursuit will bring out both of these motivations, good and bad.

The pursuit of radical life extension comes tied to a seductive half-truth—people can one day have their own version of eternal life. This kind of "eternal life" that comes through radical life extension is created on our terms, not God's terms, and culture can use it to create a false promise to people. Instead of turning their faces to heaven to seek God, people will put their hand to the plow of tech so that "whoever believes will, through technology, have radical life extension" (cf. John 3:15).

For "What good will it be for someone to gain the whole world, yet forfeit their soul?" (Matthew 16:26). What good will it be for someone to live a long time, yet forfeit their resurrection?

As a Christian, I understand God offers every person eternal life if they are willing to let God rescue them from their own self-created brokenness. That offer of eternal life is free—it comes from God's most magnanimous grace—but it is still offered on God's terms. The eternal life that transhumanism offers is a pseudo-eternal life on our own terms. Most importantly of all, radical life extension is built on healing the body, but not the soul.

We need an eternal life that is not just radical life extension but radical person restoration. We need salvation, body and soul.

ETERNALITY

As a whole, the one thing that humanity desires more than anything else is to live forever. Strikingly, of all the personal attributes of God, eternality is the one that God is willing to share with his people.[19] Humans will never be omnipotent, impassible, omniscient, or sovereign, but we will have the chance to share in God's eternity.[20]

God's eternal nature speaks first to his continual existence; at no time did God not exist, and at no time in the future will God not exist. In fact, since God created time, he exists outside of it. Time only has meaning to God in the sense that he understands it and chooses when and how he interacts with it—never in the sense that God is limited by it or bound to it. Likewise, God's eternality also reveals other important aspects of his nature. The church father Augustine speaks of God's eternality this way: "For in their own substance, by which they are, the three are one, the Father, the Son, and the Holy Spirit, the very same without any temporal movement, above every created thing, without intervals of time and place; and together they are one and the same from eternity to eternity, as it were, eternity itself, which is not without truth and charity."[21]

What this means is that because God is eternal in the way that he is eternal, God never changes who he is. That's what the Bible means when it says, "Jesus Christ is the same yesterday and today and forever" (Hebrews 13:8). It is the eternality of God that makes him always the same.

In *Self/less*, Damian Hale goes to Phoenix Biogenic because he knows that his life is coming to an end—his time is running out. When he meets Albright, the focus of the conversation and the procedure centers on the extension of Hale's life. The whole point is to give Hale more time by shedding his dying body; it is all about quantity. This is where God is totally different than we are. Because God is outside of time, God never needs more time. Therefore, everything that God focuses on is what we call quality. When God raises again those people who followed Jesus, their eternal life—like God's eternality—won't really be about the quantity of time but the quality of existence. Like God, eternal life for people in heaven will be unchangeable, meaningful, complete in every way, just as God is.

There's a bit of irony in all this: We are human beings, *Homo sapiens*. The more we use technology, and commit to technology, the more it makes us a little less human. By the time we reach the singularity, we will have consigned our bodies to a synthetic biology that literally changes who we are, from the outside in. We will look different, we will take in information differently, we will think differently. If it goes far enough, we will barely be human.

But what is the defining feature of being human? It is death. Even while we think we are becoming transhuman, and posthuman, we can never actually escape death. So in a reverse sense we are actually not becoming less human at all. Because we die—maybe at 35, maybe at 72, maybe at 120, maybe at 969, but in all cases, we die. The one thing people want the most from tech is the one thing tech will never be able to give.

There's only one way to defy death, to become posthuman, to evolve to the next stage, to gain eternal life. That doesn't come from technology.

Again, the danger, one more time: "Anyone who loves their life will lose it, while anyone who hates their life in this world will keep it for eternal life" (John 12:25).

We use our tech, but we don't put our hope in it. We live our life, but we don't put our faith in it.

THE TREE OF LIFE

When we think of heaven, we think of a paradise beyond words. We think of people, living without sorrow or sin or sadness, with the saints who have gone on before. And in the midst of it all is a God who is both love and light to everyone. In the center of that vision is the tree of life, the symbol of our partaking in eternal life with God. We know there will be God, people, other organics (trees), and inorganics (soil) in heaven. But will there be tech in heaven? Before we jump to concluding no, (or yes, for that matter), let's think through this a bit further.

Christians believe that God dwells in heaven. Christians also believe that when people who are in Christ die, those people will go to where God dwells. The common way we express this in English is to say that when Christians pass from this world, they "go to heaven," reflecting tradition and some biblical statements.[22] However, when we look at the depiction of our future home at the end of the book of Revelation, we get the impression that God's throne will remain in heaven, but that our home will be on the new—dare I say, resurrected—Earth. God's presence will come down from heaven to be with us on our new world. We will live on a renewed planet, with resurrected bodies.[23]

So, I ask again: will there be tech in heaven? The short answer is probably not. Tech is for humanity, not for God. But will there be tech on the New Earth? Yes, it sure seems that way. Think about all the streets, gates, and walls mentioned in Revelation. That's tech. In fact, these examples of tech even include dimensions, similar to the way the biblical depictions of the ark and the tabernacle also included dimensions. Maybe the "streets of gold, like transparent glass" are metaphorical, or spiritual, or allegorical, or some organic or special divine creation that just looks like a golden street; but if we go down that road, then there is no end to the reworking to which we can submit Revelation. No, in some way, for some reason, there is tech—human technology—in "heaven."

If there is a city, and walls, and gates, and streets, will there be radios, big-screen HDTVs, and smartphones in heaven, too? If we live on a renewed planet, how will we get from place to place? Walk? Fly (like the angels and birds, not on jet airliners)? Take human-constructed transportation? How will we contact other people? Smoke signals? Telepathy?

Maybe you've never thought of whether there would be tech in heaven. Maybe the idea feels disconcerting. I think it does to many people. If I ask people if their dog or cat will be in heaven, their faces will light up; if I ask the same people if their smartphones will be in heaven, I'm sure to get the opposite response. We attribute nature to God and tech to humanity.

I'm not trying to be overly speculative or make anyone feel funny. I am simply suggesting this: Revelation portrays our resurrected lives taking place on a renewed Earth, with evidence of technology present. If there is some tech present, there could be a lot of tech present. And why not? If the Earth is redeemable, and if people are redeemable, is it possible that technology can be redeemed as well?

Let's agree to discuss this further when we enter into the gates of the city and stand around the tree of life. You can bring Fluffy, and I'll bring my smartphone. Whether we have one, both, or none of these things, in the end it won't matter. On Earth, we have needed a temple to worship; but in the resurrection to come, we need no temple to worship. God and the Lamb will be our temple (see Revelation 21:22).

On Earth, we need technology to survive; but in the resurrection, we won't. On Earth, we need nature to survive, but in the resurrection, we won't. In our eternal life with God, we will eat of the fruit of the tree of life, partake directly of him, and we will thrive.

CONCLUSION
TOOLS FOR THE SANDBOX

When I applied to college, my father gave me two pieces of advice for choosing a major. The first piece of advice: "Major in engineering, especially electrical engineering. People will always need engineers." (As I mentioned earlier, he was an electrical engineer at NASA, so that advice made sense.) But his second piece of advice is what has really stayed with me all these years: "And whatever you do, don't major in computer science. Computers are going nowhere. There won't be any jobs in computers in the future."

No one said predicting the future was easy. The future is a place where angels fear to tread.

Throughout this book I have used sample technologies to illustrate how tech affects our rapidly changing world. There are many, many other technologies that we could have explored: implantable smartphones, synthetic biology, invisibility cloaks, quantum computing, 3D food printing, virtual animals, the Internet of Things, floating farms and cities, big data, and DNA storage, any of which may end up being far more world-changing than some of the ones I have included. Still, I chose the ones in this book in part because their impact is already being felt in some preliminary way, and in part because my crystal ball suggested they are destined for the greatest impact. I am fully aware that if I were writing this book in the 1970s, it would not have included the internet. Let's meet back here in forty years and see how my predictions have held up.

There are also many concerns about technology that we couldn't cover in this short book. Examples include how tech is changing our sense of privacy, how it shifts the way we look at nonhuman species, and how it will force changes in large-scale economic and political systems. We also didn't cover any potentially catastrophic scenarios, such as World War 3, an antibiotic-resistant superbug epidemic, or zombies. Any further discussion could include these issues and more. Especially zombies.

I hope that this book helped you think more deeply about tech, but even more so, I hope this book caused you to think more about God—who God is, how he relates to us, and what God *continues* to do for us, because he is not done. This will be important in the future, because the issue of how we relate to tech is not going away. In fact, technology, transhumanism, and related cultures coming from science may prove to be the biggest cultural debate of the twenty-first century.[1]

LEFT BEHIND

The future is coming. What do we do now?

One option is for the people of God to use the singularity as an exit ramp from the challenges of a futuristic world and all that it entails. Ian Curran describes what this might look like: "In a future, technologically advanced age, Christians may become a peculiar people whose primary mark of identity and means of witness is that we freely choose to live mortal lives, grow old in Christ, and die. In a world of endless virtual connections, we may choose to disconnect, knowing that our ultimate connection is with the reality of God."[2]

There is something appealing about this. It feels safe. It's like a future monasticism or the transhumanist version of the Benedict Option (a strategic withdrawal from future tech).[3] I don't believe it's wrong. I also don't believe it's best.

Christians are already peculiar people. By taking the name of Christ, we have rejected the world, even though we still have to navigate within it. Anytime that Christians are known by what worldly items or ideas we embrace or reject, we've gotten off message. Some Christians will use more tech, and some will use less; we have the freedom in Christ for our own convictions, I believe. With tech or without tech, if you're a Christian, your ultimate connection is already with God. Disconnected or not, tech has no power to change that divine connection.

I've traveled enough revolutions around the sun to know that some people don't like the future. Probably a better way of saying it is that they don't like change. For them, technology represents change, and change is uncomfortable. Instead of embracing new tech (and change), they will resist new tech (and change). If we resist future tech, we need to make sure we are resisting because it is wrong, not just because it is uncomfortable. We need to make sure that if we choose to be left behind, we won't be left out from the ways that God can use his people in this world.

BRAVING THE FUTURE TOGETHER

Today we can travel farther, communicate faster, and live longer than ever before. We are not at a place in history where tech is starting to change us; tech has already changed us. It has been changing us since the very beginning. Avoiding tech is impossible; every human uses technology. We can only avoid newer forms of tech. Instead of being left behind, as some Christians will suggest, I believe we should forge ahead. That doesn't mean we accept all tech uncritically or without boundaries. But it means that we look to future tech with the hope that it will make our world a better place.

After writing this book, I am more convinced than ever that a thoughtful Christian witness is needed to speak into the use of future tech as it arrives. Neither naïveté nor pessimism will benefit this cause. A cautious optimism will give Christians the best voice to speak truth to tech.

When my kids were a bit younger, I built a sandbox for them. I did it because my wife asked me to do so; I was actually resistant to the idea. A sandbox seemed so old-fashioned to me, and I wasn't sure anyone would use it. Yet over the years, all four of my children have played in the sandbox. A lot. They've used tools to dig holes and cut roads and make mountains. It certainly kept them occupied at key moments when bad behavior could occur instead. We have the sandbox between the door to our house and the car. If we as parents are running late, our kids can play in the sandbox while waiting to load into the car.

Sometimes I wonder if God designed the universe this way—like a sandbox, to provide his children with a place to play, discover, explore, and above all else, to keep us occupied and away from bad behavior.[4] Humanity's technologies are the tools we made for use in God's sandbox. They reveal in even finer detail a universe that God fearfully and wonderfully made, for our enjoyment and for our exploration.

I am thankful for technology. I am thankful that my children and grandchildren will likely live in a world that is healthier and safer than at any time ever before—in large part because of technology. But all this will mean nothing if they confuse the tools of the sandbox with the love of our Creator.

Want to brave the future? Know that tech will change, but God will stay the same. Your chief end is to glorify God, and to enjoy life with God forever.

FOR FURTHER READING

Campbell, Heidi A., and Stephen Garner. *Networked Theology: Negotiating Faith in Digital Culture*. Engaging Culture Series. Grand Rapids: Baker, 2016.

Detweiler, Craig. *iGods: How Technology Shapes Our Spiritual and Social Lives*. Grand Rapids: Brazos, 2013.

Dyer, John. *From the Garden to the City: The Redeeming and Corrupting Power of Technology*. Grand Rapids: Kregel, 2011.

Gingerich, Owen. *God's Universe*. Cambridge: Belknap, 2006.

Harari, Yuval Noah. *Homo Deus: A Brief History of Tomorrow*. New York: Harper, 2017.

___. *Sapiens: A Brief History of Humankind*. New York: Harper, 2015.

Jones, Mark. *God Is: A Devotional Guide to the Attributes of God*. Wheaton: Crossway, 2017.

Kelly, Kevin. *The Inevitable: Understanding the 12 Technological Forces That Will Shape Our Future*. New York: Penguin, 2017.

Sanlon, Peter. *Simply God: Recovering the Classical Trinity*. Nottingham, UK: IVP, 2017.

Shanahan, Murray. *The Technological Singularity*. MIT Press Essential Knowledge Series. Cambridge: MIT Press, 2015.

NOTES

INTRODUCTION: GOD, PEOPLE, TECH

1. One subset of modern Western culture is various groups of people who identify as Christian. Within these groups, there are those who reject an optimistic future due to their interpretation of end-times prophecies in the New Testament. This is a complex issue, but for now I simply suggest that since no one knows the time when God will wrap things up, it is possible that the world will remain optimistic about the future up until the very end (which may or may not be as soon as we think).

2. David A. Graham, "The Wrong Side of 'the Right Side of History,'" *The Atlantic*, December 21, 2015.

3. Richard A. Meckel, *Save the Babies: American Public Health Reform and the Prevention of Infant Mortality, 1850–1929* (Ann Arbor: University of Michigan, 1990), 28.

4. Ibid., 29.

5. For further discussion, see also Samuel H. Preston and Michael R. Haines, *Fatal Years: Child Mortality in Late Nineteenth-Century America* (Princeton: Princeton University Press, 2014).

6. Massimo Livi Bacci, introduction to *Infant and Child Mortality in the Past*, ed. Alain Bideau, Bertrand Desjardins, and Héctor Pérez Brignoli, International Studies in Demography (Oxford: Clarendon, 1997), 1.

7. Meckel, *Save the Babies*, 31–39.

8. Julia Sophie Woersdorfer, *The Evolution of Household Technology and Consumer Behavior, 1800–2000*, Modern Heterodox Economics (London: Routledge, 2017), 77–78, 82.

9. A futurist is a thinker or researcher who tries to predict what can happen in the future, and then makes suggestions today to encourage progress in that direction.

10. E.g., Yuval Noah Harari, *Homo Deus: A Brief History of Tomorrow* (New York: Harper, 2017), Kindle edition.

11. See Kevin Kelly, *The Inevitable: Understanding the 12 Technological Forces That Will Shape Our Future* (New York: Penguin, 2016); Simon Young, *Designer Evolution: A Transhumanist Manifesto* (Amherst: Prometheus, 2006); and cf. Fabrice Jotterand, "At the Roots of Trans-humanism: From the Enlightenment to a Post-Human Future," *Journal of Medicine and Philosophy* 35 (2010): 620.

12. Harari, *Homo Deus*, Kindle edition.

13. Benjamin Franklin, *The Works of Benjamin Franklin*, ed. Jared Sparks, vol. 6 (Chicago: Townsend Mac Coun, 1882), 382–83.

14. Andy Crouch, *The Tech-Wise Family: Everyday Steps for Putting Technology in Its Proper Place* (Grand Rapids: Baker, 2017); and Brian Housman, *Tech Savvy Parenting: Navigating Your Child's Digital Life* (Nashville: Randall House, 2014).

15. Readers may recognize that all eight of these listed are attributes of God and God alone. Because one of my arguments in this book is that people will try to use tech to set themselves up as gods, I thought it best to focus the theological contrast to theology proper (who God is). If we better understand who God is, we will better grasp why people cannot, and will never, be gods.

16. Tony Davies, *Humanism*, The New Critical Idiom (London: Routledge, 1997), 26.

17. Harari, *Homo Deus*, Kindle edition.

18. Hava Tirosh-Samuelson and Kenneth L. Mossman, "New Perspectives on Transhumanism," in *Building Better Humans? Refocusing the Debate on Transhumanism*, ed. Hava Tirosh-Samuelson and Kenneth L. Mossman, Beyond Humanism: Trans- and Posthumanism 3 (Frankfurt am Main: Peter Lang, 2011), 37.

19. Mark Walker, "Transhumanism," in *What the Future Looks Like: Scientists Predict the Next Great Discoveries and Reveal How Today's Breakthroughs Are Already Shaping Our World*, ed. Jim Al-Khalili (New York: The Experiment, 2018), 96.

20. Julian Huxley, *New Bottles for New Wine* (London: Chatto & Windus, 1957), 17.

21. Andrea Vicini and Agnes M. Brazal, "Longing for Transcendence: Cyborgs and Trans- and Posthumans," *Theological Studies* 76 (2015): 157.

22. See Jonathan Edwards, "Sinners in the Hands of an Angry God," sermon given July 8, 1741, Enfield, Connecticut, and Joel Osteen, *Your Best Life Now: 7 Steps to Living at Your Full Potential*, updated ed. (New York: FaithWords, 2014).

1 READY PLAYER ONE

1. For further discussion on the role of avatars, see Douglas Estes, *SimChurch: Being the Church in the Virtual World* (Grand Rapids: Zondervan, 2008).

2. Ernest Cline, *Ready Player One: A Novel* (New York: Crown, 2011). In the book haptic gloves provide realistic touch and precision motion tracking in VR.

3. Peter Rubin, *Future Presence: How Virtual Reality Is Changing Human Connection, Intimacy, and the Limits of Ordinary Life* (New York: HarperOne, 2018), 6–7.

4. John Koetsier, "VR Needs More Social: 77% of Virtual Reality Users Want More Social Engagement," *Forbes*, April 30, 2018.

5. Rubin, *Future Presence*, 8.

6. Similarly, Charlie Brooker, the creator of the popular sci-fi TV series, *Black Mirror*, notes that tech "does feel like a drug," in "The Dark Side of Our Gadget Addiction," *The Guardian*, December 1, 2011.

7 See dscout, "Mobile Touches: A Study on Humans and Their Tech," published as blog post on dscout.com, June 16, 2016; Mark Nicas and Daniel Best, "A Study Quantifying the Hand-to-Face Contact Rate and Its Potential Application to Predicting Respiratory Tract Infection," *Journal of Occupational and Environmental Hygiene* 5 (2008): 347–52; and Echo Research, *2009 National Clean Hands Report Card* (Washington, DC: American Cleaning Institute, 2009), respectively.

8. Abigail Abrams, "Your Cell Phone Is 10 Times Dirtier Than a Toilet Seat: Here's What to Do About It," *Time*, August 23, 2017.

9. For a lengthier discussion, see Leo Marx and Merritt Roe Smith, introduction to *Does Technology Drive History? The Dilemma of Technological Determinism*, ed. Merritt Roe Smith and Leo Marx (Cambridge: MIT Press, 1994).

10. We can find a list of components necessary to create the tech in the 14th century BC Ugaritic text *The Legend of Aqhat*; see Simon B. Parker, ed., *Ugaritic Narrative Poetry*, SBL Writings from the Ancient World 9 (Atlanta: Scholars, 1997).

11. See Mike Loades, *The Composite Bow* (Oxford: Osprey, 2016).

12. Daniel R. Hedrick, *Technology: A World History* (Oxford: Oxford University Press, 2009), 74.

13. Dan Brendsel (PhD, Wheaton), a minister to college students and young adults at Grace Church of DuPage, pointed out to me that even if many Christian scholars are determinist, the average person in our world is instrumentalist—mostly due to not thinking too much about tech and a love for gadgets. In light of this, it becomes even

more imperative that our love for gadgets never overtakes wise and healthy living.

14. As Steven J. Jensen says so well, "It is not so much the technologies—whether real or imagined—that are problematic; it is the attitudes that necessarily underlie the use of these technologies," from his essay, "The Roots of Transhumanism," *Nova et Vetera* (English Edition) 12 (2014): 516.

15. Lee Moran, "Seattle Eatery in War of Words with Customer Booted for Wearing Google Glass," *New York Daily News*, November 29, 2013.

16. It seems to me that instrumentalism makes the better case for this than determinism.

17. This is a common theme in mildly dystopian sci-fi movies such as *Elysium*.

18. William Lane Craig, *God Over All: Divine Aseity and the Challenge of Platonism* (Oxford: Oxford University Press, 2016), 1.

19. Bob Doede, "Transhumanism, Technology, and the Future: Posthumanity Emerging or Sub-Humanity Descending?" *Appraisal* 7:3 (2009): 52.

2 REAL STEEL

1. A film based on the screenplay by John Gatins, Dan Gilroy, and Jeremy Leven, from the original short story by Richard Matheson. See Richard Matheson, "Steel," in *Steel: And Other Stories* (New York: Tor, 2011).

2. Will Knight, "This Is How the Robot Uprising Finally Begins," *MIT Technology Review*, June 25, 2018.

3. John Markoff, "Planes Without Pilots," *New York Times*, April 6, 2015.

4. National Highway Traffic Safety Administration, "2016 Quick Facts," (2017): 1.

5. For a contrary position, see Nigel M. De S. Cameron, *Will Robots Take Your Job? A Plea for Consensus* (Cambridge: Polity, 2017).

6. Pope John Paul II, *Laborem exercens*, 6.

7. Ideas distilled from arguments by Darrell Cosden, *A Theology of Work: Work and the New Creation*, Paternoster Theological Monographs (Milton Keynes, UK: Paternoster, 2004); and Miroslav Volf, *Work in the Spirit: Toward a Theology of Work* (Oxford: Oxford University Press, 1991).

8. For example, modern medicine has provided us with a richer view of the beginning and end of human life.

9. Yuval Noah Harari, *Sapiens: A Brief History of Humankind* (New York: HarperCollins, 2015), 82.

10. One of the goals of transhumanism is happiness, which transhumanists believe will come through the use of advanced tech; see Hava Tirosh-Samuelson and Kenneth L. Mossman, "New Perspectives on Transhumanism," in *Building Better Humans? Refocusing the Debate on Transhumanism*, ed. Hava Tirosh-Samuelson and Kenneth L. Mossman, Beyond Humanism: Trans- and Posthumanism 3 (Frankfurt am Main: Peter Lang, 2011), 35.

11. See Douglas Estes, "Does 'The Image of God' Extend to Robots, Too?" *Christianity Today*, February 27, 2017.

12. For a similar definition, see Richard E. Creel, *Divine Impassibility: An Essay in Philosophical Theology* (Cambridge: Cambridge University Press, 1985).

13. J. I. Packer, "What Do You Mean When You Say God?" *Christianity Today* (September 10, 1986): 31.

14. In this I use the concept of flourishing from a human perspective. Again, the goal of life for the Christian is to be blessed by God, which comes through obedience.

15. Julian Huxley, *New Bottles for New Wine* (London: Chatto & Windus, 1957), 17.

3 JURASSIC WORLD

1. Robin George Andrews, "How to Train Your Velociraptor, 'Jurassic World' Style," *Discover*, June 14, 2015.

2. Tanya Lewis, "Woolly Mammoth DNA Inserted into Elephant Cells," *Live Science*, March 26, 2015.

3. Michael Greshko, "Sheep-Human Hybrids Made in Lab—Get the Facts," *National Geographic*, February 18, 2018.

4. Antonio Regalado, "First Gene-Edited Dogs Reported in China," *MIT Technology Review*, October 19, 2015.

5. David Cyranoski, "Gene-edited 'Micropigs' To Be Sold as Pets at Chinese Institute," *Nature* 526 (2015): 18.

6. David P. Barash, "It's Time to Make Human-Chimp Hybrids," *Nautilus*, March 8, 2018.

7. *WIRED* magazine produced a cool video that explains CRISPR gene editing using Thomas the Tank Engine-style pieces: http://video.wired .com/watch/crispr-gene-editing-explained.

8. Johnny H. Hu et al., "Evolved Cas9 Variants with Broad PAM Compatibility and High DNA Specificity," *Nature* 556 (2018): 57–63.

9. Jane E. Brody, "Are G.M.O. Foods Safe?" *New York Times*, April 23, 2018.

10. Emma Harris, "Process of Elimination," *WIRED*, February 28, 2018.

11. For a similar take by a different environmental scientist, see Jeremy Lederhouse, "Christians, Think Twice about Eradicating Mosquitoes to Defeat Malaria," *Christianity Today*, April 25, 2017.

12. Giovanni Papini, "What Pragmatism is Like," *Popular Science Monthly* 71 (1907): 353.

13. Note the ideas, and even the journal's title, in Papini, "What Pragmatism is Like," 351.

14. Matthew Moss, "The Story of the Gatling Gun," *Popular Mechanics*, August 22, 2016.

15. Julian Quinones and Arijeta Lajka, "'What Kind of Society Do You Want To Live In?': Inside the Country Where Down Syndrome Is Disappearing," *CBS News*, August 14, 2017.

16. For example, Ilona Amos, "Scottish GM Crops Ban to Have 'Apocalyptic' Effect," *The Scotsman*, August 15, 2015; but not to be confused with the precautionary principle, which is the idea that tech advance must follow adequate precautions, placing the burden of proof on the advance not the skeptic.

17. Abby Norman, "A New Test Can Read Your Future Child's Genome While They're Still in the Womb," *Futurism*, February 9, 2018.

18. Mark Walker, "Transhumanism," in *What the Future Looks Like: Scientists Predict the Next Great Discoveries and Reveal How Today's Breakthroughs Are Already Shaping Our World*, ed. Jim Al-Khalili (New York: The Experiment, 2018), 86.

19. See Douglas Estes, "Sin and the Cyborg: On the (Im)Peccability of the Posthuman," *Bulletin for Ecclesial Theology*, forthcoming.

20. For one of the earliest stories that sparked interest, see Jason G. Goldman, "Man's New Best Friend? A Forgotten Russian Experiment in Fox Domestication," *Scientific American*, September 6, 2010.

21. Lee Alan Dugatkin and Lyudmila Trut, *How to Tame a Fox (and Build a Dog): Visionary Scientists and a Siberian Tale of Jump-Started Evolution* (Chicago: University of Chicago Press, 2017), 12.

22. O. Carter Snead, "The Alfie Evans Case is Straight Out of a Dystopia," *CNN*, April 29, 2018.

23. Jonathan Edwards, *The Works of Jonathan Edwards* (Edinburgh: Banner of Truth Trust, 1974), 1:681.

24. Giovanni Pico della Mirandola, *Oration on the Dignity of Man*, trans. A. Robert Gaponigri (Washington, DC: Regnery, 2012).

25. A precursor to this use occurs in Isaiah 1:6.

4 PASSENGERS

1. Siri already does basically the same thing; see Jonathan Merritt, "Is AI a Threat to Christianity?" *The Atlantic*, February 3, 2017.

2. Peter Dockrill, "In Just 4 Hours, Google's AI Mastered All the Chess Knowledge in History," *ScienceAlert*, December 7, 2017.

3. For a longer explanation, see Kate Baggaley, "There Are Two Kinds of AI, and the Difference Is Important," *Popular Science*, February 23, 2017; or Ben Dickson, "What is Narrow, General and Super Artificial Intelligence?" *TechTalks*, May 12, 2017.

4. Douglas Estes, "You Have Searched Me, Oh Apple Face ID, and You Know Me," *Christianity Today*, April 5, 2018.

5. James Vincent, "Google's New AI Algorithm Predicts Heart Disease by Looking at Your Eyes," *The Verge*, February 19, 2018.

6. Ming Ming Chiu, Kathryn C. Seigfried-Spellar, and Tatiana R. Ringenberg, "Exploring Detection of Contact vs. Fantasy Online Sexual Offenders in Chats with Minors: Statistical Discourse Analysis of Self-Disclosure and Emotion Words," *Child Abuse and Neglect* 81 (2018): 128–38.

7. Emerging Technology from the arXiv, "A Machine Has Figured out Rubik's Cube All by Itself," *MIT Technology Review*, June 15, 2018; and Kollen Post, "Forget Chess: Artificial Intelligence Is Now Debating People," *Science*, June 21, 2018.

8. This is an idea popularized by Pedro Domingos in his book, *The Master Algorithm: How the Quest for the Ultimate Learning Machine Will Remake Our World* (New York: Basic, 2015).

9. See Jolene Creighton, "The 'Father of Artificial Intelligence' Says Singularity Is 30 Years Away," *Futurism*, February 14, 2018; and Corey Pein, "The Singularity is Not Near: The Intellectual Fraud of the 'Singularitarians,'" *Salon*, May 13, 2018.

10. Murray Shanahan, *The Technological Singularity*, MIT Press Essential Knowledge Series (Cambridge: MIT Press, 2015), xv.

11. That's the popular take on Nietzsche, not his actual argument.

12. See David Mattin, "Stop Waiting for the Singularity. It Started 200 Years Ago," *NewCo Shift*, March 7, 2018.

13. For an example of this, see H. G. Wells, *Science and the World-Mind* (London: New Europe Publishing Company, 1942), 31.

14. For a visual sense of "romance," see Caspar David Friedrich's 1818 painting, *Wanderer above the Sea of Fog*.

15. However, I argue there will always be mysteries in our world; they will appear as the inverse of the exponential curve.

16. Herman Bavinck, *Reformed Dogmatics, Vol 2: God and Creation*, ed. John Bolt, trans. John Vriend (Grand Rapids: Baker, 2004), 196.

17. For more information, see David E. Aune, "Divination," in *The International Standard Bible Encyclopedia*, ed. Geoffrey W. Bromiley, rev. ed. (Grand Rapids: Eerdmans, 1979–1988), 1:971–74.

5 MARJORIE PRIME

1. William James, *The Principles of Psychology* (New York: Henry Holt and Company, 1890), 1:648.

2. A RAID is a redundant backup utilizing multiple hard drives. Today they are inexpensive, and one of the best ways to protect digital photos, keepsakes, and documents.

3. For a more in-depth explanation, see the introduction to *Brain-Computer Interfaces: Principles and Practice*, ed. Jonathan R. Wolpaw and Elizabeth Winter Wolpaw (Oxford: Oxford University Press, 2012).

4. Adapted and expanded from the introduction to *Brain-Computer Interfaces*, 4–5.

5. Simon Makin, "Brain-Computer Interface Allows Speediest Typing to Date," *Scientific American*, February 21, 2017.

6. Emily Mullin, "For Brain-Computer Interfaces to Be Useful, They'll Need to Be Wireless," *MIT Technology Review*, November 8, 2017.

7. Here I am reminded of the view of some traditional peoples, who believe that a digital camera can capture the soul of a person. I personally met a few people in rural East Africa who held this belief to some degree.

8. For discussion, see Paul Root Wolpe, "A Human Head Transplant Would Be Reckless and Ghastly. It's Time to Talk about It," *Vox*, June 12, 2018.

9. Antonio Regalado, "Researchers Are Keeping Pig Brains Alive Outside the Body," *MIT Technology Review*, April 25, 2018.

10. Cf., Marlowe Hood, "Sweeping Gene Survey Reveals New Facets of Evolution," *Phys.org*, May 28, 2018.

11. For an extended retelling of this story, see Yuval Noah Harari, *Sapiens: A Brief History of Humankind* (New York: HarperCollins, 2015). There are other versions of this story, each as well-articulated as the next; see for example, Byron Reese, *The Fourth Age: Smart Robots, Conscious Computers and the Future of Humanity* (New York: Atria, 2018).

12. From the song "Material Girl," popularized by Madonna and written by Peter Brown and Robert Rans; released January 23, 1985.

13. For a brief overview, see Michael Burdett, "The Image of God and Evolution," in *Finding Ourselves after Darwin: Conversations on the Image of God, Original Sin, and the Problem of Evil*, ed. Stanley P. Rosenberg (Grand Rapids: Baker, 2018), 27–31.

14. For further discussion, see Joshua R. Farris, "Souls and Bodies: Why We Still Matter," *Didaktikos* 2:2 (2018): 42–44.

15. Perhaps even more if our bodies are burned to ash or donated to science.

16. Ted Peters, "The Soul of Trans-Humanism," *Dialog* 44 (2005): 381–95.

17. Kevin Rawlinson, "Seven-Year-Old Boy Recovering Well After Five-Organ Transplant," *The Guardian*, April 24, 2018.

18. Eugene Clay, "Transhumanism and the Orthodox Christian Tradition," in *Building Better Humans? Refocusing the Debate on Transhumanism*, ed. Hava Tirosh-Samuelson and Kenneth L. Mossman, Beyond Humanism: Trans- and Posthumanism 3 (Frankfurt am Main: Peter Lang, 2011), 159.

19. Mark Robert Anderson, "Twenty Years On from Deep Blue vs Kasparov: How a Chess Match Started the Big Data Revolution," *The Conversation*, May 11, 2017.

20. Brad Bush, "How Combined Human and Computer Intelligence Will Redefine Jobs," *TechCrunch*, November 1, 2016.

21. I mean "successful" here as a shorthand for "successful in God's eyes," in the sense that God often calls believers to various sacrifices that can look rather "unsuccessful" if judged only by the world's external evaluations.

22. In Christian theology, the two ways people get at knowledge of God is through general revelation and special revelation.

23. Steven J. Kraftchick, "Plac'd on this Isthmus of a Middle State: Reflections on Psalm 8 and Human Becoming," *Word & World* 35 (2015): 118.

24. Of course, people in earlier times could have benefited from a deeper reading of Scripture. But Christendom (Christians as a powerful political majority in the West) obscured many of the problems, such that the average Christian could hide behind a dominant reading of the Bible that circulated in culture.

25. Wolfhart Pannenberg, *Systematic Theology* (Grand Rapids: Eerdmans, 1991), 1:410.

26. What about time machines? I do believe that time travel is possible, at least as I understand and accept Minkowski spacetime. However, time travel is so far out on the exponential curve that I have a hard time believing it will come to pass before God decides to wrap things up and call it a day (the consummation of the ages). Still, even if God

waits until after we develop time travel, it does not invalidate my argument because human travel (and thus knowledge) will always be within spacetime, which means we can never fully see or understand first causes (for example, the Big Bang).

27. Karl Barth, *Church Dogmatics: The Doctrine of God*, Volume 2, Part 1, ed. G. W. Bromiley and T. F. Torrance, trans. T. H. L. Parker et al. (London: T&T Clark, 1957), 463–64.

28. Isabel Kershner, "A Carved Stone Block Upends Assumptions about Ancient Judaism," *New York Times*, December 8, 2015.

29. Leslie C. Allen, *Ezekiel 1–19*, Word Biblical Commentary 28 (Dallas: Word, 1998), 34.

6 ROBOT & FRANK

1. See Matt Simon, "What Is a Robot?" *WIRED*, August 24, 2017.

2. A clepsydra is an ancient time-measuring device, and a capacitor is an energy storage device.

3. Jamie Condliffe, "What Happens When Robots Become Role Models," *MIT Technology Review*, February 22, 2017.

4. Especially if we take the approach that people are composed of three parts: body, soul, and spirit (see 1 Thessalonians 5:23; Hebrews 4:12). If this were true, it may be possible to speak of robots as having a type of soul (as we speak of animals as having a type of soul), but without a spirit (and without the Holy Spirit). As you can see, there are several variables at work in this discussion!

5. Isobel Asher Hamilton, "People Kicking These Food Delivery Robots Is an Early Insight into How Cruel Humans Could Be to Robots," *Business Insider*, June 9, 2018.

6. Xanthe Mallett, "No Evidence that Sexbots Reduce Harms to Women and Children," *The Conversation*, June 5, 2018.

7. Douglas Estes, "Does 'The Image of God' Extend to Robots, Too?" *Christianity Today*, February 27, 2017.

8. Robert Ranisch and Stefan Lorenz Sorgner, "Introducing Post- and Transhumanism," in *Post- and Transhumanism: An Introduction*, ed. Robert Ranisch and Stefan Lorenz Sorgner, Beyond Humanism 1 (Frankfurt am Main: Peter Lang, 2014), 10.

9. Micha Brumlik, "Transhumanism Is Humanism, and Humanism Is Transhumanism," in *Perfecting Human Futures: Transhuman Visions and Technological Imaginations*, ed. J. Benjamin Hurlbut and Hava Tirosh-Samuelson, Futures of Technology, Science and Society (Berlin: Springer, 2016), 121; Cary Wolfe, *What is Posthumanism?* Posthumanities 8 (Minneapolis: University of Minnesota Press, 2010), xv; and

Nick Bostrom et al., "The Transhumanist FAQ," in *Transhumanism and the Body: The World Religions Speak*, ed. Calvin Mercer and Derek F. Maher (New York: Palgrave Macmillan, 2014), 1.

10. For an historical overview, see Lewis W. Spitz, "Humanism," in *Encyclopedia of Religion*, ed. Lindsay Jones, 2nd ed. (Detroit: Thomson Gale, 2005), 4174–78.

11. Konstantin Kolenda, "Humanism," in *The Cambridge Dictionary of Philosophy*, ed. Robert Audi, 2nd ed. (Cambridge: Cambridge University Press, 1999), 396–97; and Andrew Copson, "What Is Humanism?" in *The Wiley Blackwell Handbook of Humanism*, ed. Andrew Copson and A. C. Grayling (Oxford: Wiley Blackwell, 2015), 4; respectively.

12. Within the soft form of humanism there exists even a "Christian humanism." It's complicated, as on one hand some humanists suggest Christian humanism is not possible, and on the other hand some Christians also suggest it is not possible, for contrastive reasons. However, I admit that I am supportive of Christian humanism. I feel that it is an ism that can be compatible in some ways with Christian theology and practice.

13. Charles T. Rubin, *Eclipse of Man: Human Extinction and the Meaning of Progress* (New York: New Atlantis, 2014), Kindle edition.

14. David S. Oderberg, "Could There Be a Superhuman Species?" *Southern Journal of Philosophy* 52 (2014): 206; and Philip Hefner, "The Animal That Aspires to Be an Angel: The Challenges of Transhumanism," *Dialog* 48 (2009): 164–73.

15. Just as Christian humanism has arisen alongside a soft form of humanism, so too has Christian transhumanism arisen alongside a soft form of transhumanism. Currently, one of the most outspoken advocates of this pairing is Christopher Benek, founder of the Christian Transhumanist Association; see Brandon Showalter, "Artificial Intelligence, Transhumanism and the Church: How Should Christians Respond?" *Christian Post*, January 27, 2018. I am sympathetic to Benek's posture, yet the newness of transhumanism means its trajectory is not well determined. Maybe this is an opportunity for Christians to engage.

16. At present this appears to be a very small group, but one whose power is amplified by the internet; see Hava Tirosh-Samuelson, "Transhumanism as a Secularist Faith," *Zygon* 47 (2012): 717.

17. Linell E. Cady, "Religion and the Technowonderland of Transhumanism," in *Building Better Humans? Refocusing the Debate on Transhumanism*, ed. Hava Tirosh-Samuelson and Kenneth L. Mossman, Beyond Humanism: Trans- and Posthumanism 3 (Frankfurt am Main: Peter Lang, 2011), 88.

18. From the song "Heaven is a Place on Earth," popularized by Belinda Carlisle and written by Rick Nowels and Ellen Shipley; released September 1987.

19. Cady, "Religion and the Technowonderland of Transhumanism," 83.

20. For a similar conclusion, see Calvin Mercer, "Bodies and Persons: Theological Reflections on Transhumanism," *Dialog* 54 (2015): 31.

21. Mikhail Epstein, "Technology as a New Theology From 'New Atheism' to Technotheism," in *Evolution and the Future: Anthropology, Ethics, Religion*, ed. Stefan Lorenz Sorgner and Branka-Rista Jovanovic, with Nikola Grimm, Beyond Humanism: Trans- and Posthumanism 5 (Frankfurt am Main: Peter Lang, 2013), 128.

22. This is my paraphrase of the story; see Genesis 1:27, 6:5; Romans 1:16-17, 5:8; Colossians 1:20-22, John 1:12, 14:6; Revelation 21:1-2; respectively.

23. See, for example, Luke 4:36; John 4:48, 11:42.

24. This is my paraphrase of the story repeated (in various degrees) throughout transhumanist literature.

25. Cf. Ted Peters, "Progress and Provolution: Will Transhumanism Leave Sin Behind?" in *Transhumanism and Transcendence: Christian Hope in an Age of Technological Enhancement*, ed. Ronald Cole-Turner (Washington, DC: Georgetown University Press, 2011), 66; and Olivier Masson, "Turning into Gods: Transhumanist Insight on Tomorrow's Religiosity," *Implicit Religion* 17 (2014): 445.

26. Even back in the 1980s, it was clear that some projects were made by students and some were made by parents. Some were thrown together, and some were bought with serious money. After seeing the wide variety in quality at my first one, my dad got in his mind that I was going to build something spectacular next time around. On these challenges, see Hana Schank, "Science Fairs Aren't So Fair," *The Atlantic*, March 12, 2015.

27. Thomas F. Torrance, *The Christian Doctrine of God, One Being Three Persons* (Edinburgh: T&T Clark, 1996), 204.

28. Likewise, the Bible describes both God's Son, Jesus, and God's Spirit as holy (see John 6:69, 14:26; Acts 2:27, 3:14). This reveals that the Father, Son, and Spirit are of one nature, and united in their almighty power. On Earth, Jesus demonstrated how we are to live in respect to power (see Philippians 2:5-8).

29. Cf. Origen, *First Principles*, 1.2.10.

30. Carl F. H. Henry, *God, Revelation, and Authority*, 2nd ed. (Wheaton: Crossway, 1999), 5:307.

31. Cf. Brian Patrick Green, "Transhumanism and Roman Catholicism: Imagined and Real Tensions," *Theology and Science* 13 (2015): 193.

32. For background discussion, see Craig S. Keener, *The Gospel of John: A Commentary* (Peabody: Hendrickson, 2003), 1:779–81.

33. Tacitus, *Histories*, 4.81.

34. The question arises as to whether Vespasian's (and Jesus') use of spit was more grounded in their culture's understanding of magic more than medicine. In the ancient world, there was much greater fluidity between magic and medicine than how we would view it today. Or, for a modern take, in a quote attributed to the sci-fi writer Arthur C. Clarke: "Magic's just science that we don't understand yet."

7 TRANSCENDENCE

1. Chris Phoenix and Eric Drexler, "Safe Exponential Manufacturing," *Nanotechnology* 15 (2004): 869–72.

2. Andrew Masterson, "Carnivorous Plant Inspires Nanotech Blood Cleanser," *Cosmos*, February 7, 2018.

3. The prototype under commercial development uses a small, solar-powered fan to accelerate the speed of catching water, though the net will work without the fan; see Eric Betz, "A Nanotech Device Harvests Water in the Driest Places," *Discover*, March 6, 2018.

4. Jim Handy, "How Big is a Nanometer?" *Forbes*, December 14, 2011.

5. Amretashis Sengupta and Chandan Kumar Sarkar, introduction to *Introduction to Nano: Basics to Nanoscience and Nanotechnology*, ed. Amretashis Sengupta and Chandan Kumar Sarkar, Engineering Materials (Berlin: Springer, 2015), 2.

6. Steven A. Edwards, *The Nanotech Pioneers: Where Are They Taking Us?* (Weinheim: Wiley-VCH, 2006), 1.

7. Murray Shanahan, *The Technological Singularity*, MIT Press Essential Knowledge Series (Cambridge: MIT Press, 2015), 26.

8. Terry Devitt, "Religion Colors Americans' Views of Nanotechnology," *EurekAlert*, February 15, 2008.

9. Linell E. Cady, "Religion and the Technowonderland of Transhumanism," in *Building Better Humans? Refocusing the Debate on Transhumanism*, ed. Hava Tirosh-Samuelson and Kenneth L. Mossman, Beyond Humanism: Trans- and Posthumanism 3 (Frankfurt am Main: Peter Lang, 2011), 92.

10. For a popular treatment on the relationship between power and our calling as Christians, see Andy Crouch, *Playing God: Redeeming the Gift of Power* (Grand Rapids: IVP, 2013).

11. Cf. Ted Peters, "The Soul of Trans-Humanism," *Dialog* 44 (2005): 383.

12. For example, Steven J. Jensen, "The Roots of Transhumanism," *Nova et Vetera* (English Edition) 12 (2014): 519.

13. For a similar take, see Joel Thompson, "Transhumanism: How Far Is Too Far?" *New Bioethics* 23 (2017): 166.

14. For an overview of the weakness of the cure/enhancement distinction, see Ronald Cole-Turner, introduction to *Transhumanism and Transcendence: Christian Hope in an Age of Technological Enhancement*, ed. Ronald Cole-Turner (Washington, DC: Georgetown University Press, 2011), 3–4.

15. James P. Freeman, "Word Wise: Biohacking," *Inside Sources*, June 13, 2018.

16. Ronald Bailey, "Adventures in Home Biohacking with CRISPR," *Reason*, July 2018.

17. For a popular-level approach to this, see, for example, Jacqueline Detwiler, "I Hacked My Body So You Don't Have To," *Popular Mechanics*, June 25, 2018.

18. Moa Petersén, "Thousands of Swedes Are Inserting Microchips into Themselves—Here's Why," *The Conversation*, June 20, 2018.

19. Kristen V. Brown, "I Spent a Weekend with Cyborgs, and Now I Have an RFID Implant I Have No Idea What to Do With," *Gizmodo*, April 29, 2018.

20. *Theosis* in Christian theology is a rich concept that is not easily translated into English. The concept includes the movement and perfection of people toward God, but based on God's intimacy with his people. In this idea, people become divine because they are taking part in who God is and what he is doing; for example, see Johannes Panagopoulos and Veli-Matti Kärkkäinen, "Theosis," in *The Encyclopedia of Christianity*, ed. Erwin Fahlbusch et al. (Grand Rapids: Eerdmans, 2008), 5:452–55.

21. Hava Tirosh-Samuelson and Kenneth L. Mossman, "New Perspectives on Transhumanism," in *Building Better Himans? Refocussing the Debate on Transhumanism*, ed. Hava Tirosh-Samuelson and Kenneth L. Mossman, Beyond Humanism: Trans- and Posthumanism 3 (Frankfurt am Main: Peter Lang, 2011), 29.

22. Paavan Mathema and Annabel Symington, "Mount Everest, the High-Altitude Rubbish Dump," *Agence France Presse*, June 17, 2018.

23. Perhaps a better word for my father's worldview is *scientism*; for a description, see Maarten Boudry and Massimo Pigliucci, introduction to *Science Unlimited? The Challenges of Scientism*, ed. Maarten Boudry and Massimo Pigliucci (Chicago: University of Chicago Press, 2017), Kindle edition.

24. Brian Patrick Green, "Transhumanism and Roman Catholicism: Imagined and Real Tensions," *Theology and Science* 13 (2015): 191.

25. Cf. Cady, "Religion and the Technowonderland of Transhumanism," 87.

26. From the theology of "Lola," a song written by Ray Davies, performed by the Kinks, and released on June 12, 1970.

27. From the movie *Bill and Ted's Excellent Adventure*, written by Chris Matheson and Ed Solomon, directed by Stephen Herek, and released 1989.

28. Jerome, *Dogmatic and Polemical Works*, trans. John N. Hritzu, Fathers of the Church 53 (Washington, DC: Catholic University of America Press, 1965), 252–57.

29. Hazel W. Perkin, "Cloth, Cloth Manufacturing," in *Baker Encyclopedia of the Bible*, ed. Walter A. Elwell (Grand Rapids: Baker, 1988), 1:482.

30. G. L. Borchert, "Laodicea," in *The International Standard Bible Encyclopedia*, ed. Geoffrey W. Bromiley, rev. ed. (Grand Rapids: Eerdmans, 1979–1988), 3:72–74.

8 SELF/LESS

1. The frog in a pot story is a myth, though an enduring one; see Fast Company, "Next Time, What Say We Boil a Consultant," *Fast Company*, October 31, 1995.

2. The word first appears in Manfred E. Clynes and Nathan S. Kline, "Cyborgs and Space," *Astronautics*, September 1960.

3. Garfield Benjamin, *The Cyborg Subject: Reality, Consciousness, Parallax* (London: Palgrave Macmillan, 2016), 3.

4. D. A. Novikov, *Cybernetics: From Past to Future*, Studies in Systems, Decision and Control 47 (Berlin: Springer, 2016), 1–2. Technically, cybernetics includes technology that can also control societal functions, but here we focus simply on the popular-level understanding. For the work that launched the field, see Norbert Wiener, *Cybernetics: Or, Control and Communication in the Animal and the Machine*, 2nd ed. (Cambridge: MIT Press, 1961).

5. Benjamin, *Cyborg Subject*, viii.

6. Dyllan Furness, "Who Controls the Tech Inside Us?" *Digital Trends*, July 4, 2018.

7. Nick Cowen, "We Talk to the World's First Cyborg . . . and He Can Hear Colours," *The Citizen*, May 7, 2018.

8. See, for example, Arthur Kroker, *Exits to the Posthuman Future* (Cambridge: Polity, 2014), 95–96.

9. For the record, I typically play classical civilizations, like Greece, with a wonder-builder strategy.

10. See, for example, Andrea Vicini and Agnes M. Brazal, "Longing for Transcendence: Cyborgs and Trans- and Posthumans," *Theological Studies* 76 (2015): 161.

11. Cf. Richard Saage, "New Man in Utopian and Transhumanist Perspective," *European Journal of Futures Research* 1 (2013): 14.

12. William J. Mitchell, *Me++: The Cyborg Self and the Networked City* (Cambridge: MIT Press, 2003), 168.

13. For transhumanists, it is the fountain of youth; for humanists, it is true love. See how that works?

14. Hava Tirosh-Samuelson and Kenneth L. Mossman, "New Perspectives on Transhumanism," in *Building Better Humans? Refocusing the Debate on Transhumanism*, ed. Hava Tirosh-Samuelson and Kenneth L. Mossman, Beyond Humanism: Trans- and Posthumanism 3 (Frankfurt am Main: Peter Lang, 2011), 29.

15. Vicini and Brazal, "Longing for Transcendence," 164.

16. Scholars estimate the infant mortality rate in the ancient world was about thirty times higher that it is in the United States today; see Mary Harlow and Ray Laurence, *Growing Up and Growing Old in Ancient Rome: A Life Course Approach* (New York: Routledge, 2002), 8.

17. Some Christians may wonder how my views of life extension square with my reading of Genesis 6:3, which says, "Then the Lord said, 'My Spirit will not contend with humans forever, for they are mortal; their days will be a hundred and twenty years.'" It is an interesting statement on several levels, and a full discussion is beyond the scope of this simple note. I will mention a few thoughts briefly. First, for most of human history, the lives of humans were not even close to 120 years. Second, if we try to interpret it as some upper limit that applies to us today, we would need to argue that the passage is broadly prophetic and try to figure out how it would apply to humans who already have lived beyond 120 years. Third, it is important we don't pull it out of its context: notably, this is God's response to "sons of God" taking human women as wives. This must be factored in, which invalidates using it as a general proof text against life extension. This is a difficult statement, but in my reading, it appears to be focused more on how different groups in the world relate to each other rather than a modern life-expectancy maximum.

18. Brian Patrick Green, "Transhumanism and Roman Catholicism: Imagined and Real Tensions," *Theology and Science* 13 (2015): 188.

19. The eternality of God is qualitatively different than the eternality of people, so I make this statement from the perspective of people (not an absolute statement about God). From the perspective of our limited horizon, our eternality feels similar to God's eternality.

20. Conceivably, we may participate in God's other attributes by virtue of relationship, but as in the previous note, I am speaking from a human perspective.

21. Augustine, *The Trinity*, 4.21.30, McKenna.

22. See, for example, Ephesians 2:6; Philippians 3:20; 1 Thessalonians 4:17; 2 Timothy 4:18.

23. Recent scholarship supports this general conclusion; see, for example, J. Richard Middleton, *A New Heaven and a New Earth: Reclaiming Biblical Eschatology* (Grand Rapids: Baker, 2014).

CONCLUSION

1. Mark Walker, "Transhumanism," in *What the Future Looks Like: Scientists Predict the Next Great Discoveries and Reveal How Today's Breakthroughs Are Already Shaping Our World*, ed. Jim Al-Khalili (New York: The Experiment, 2018), 96.

2. Ian Curran, "Becoming Godlike?" *Christian Century*, November 22, 2017.

3. The Benedict Option suggests Christians make a strategic withdrawal from the decline of Western culture; the "transhumanist" version of this would be Christians who strategically withdraw from the use of technology. See Rod Dreher, *The Benedict Option: A Strategy for Christians in a Post-Christian Nation* (New York: Sentinel, 2017).

4. Douglas Estes, "The Exoplanets Declare the Glory of God," *Christianity Today*, March 14, 2017.

INDEX

THE AUTHOR

Douglas Estes is associate professor
of New Testament and practical
theology at South University. Estes
has pastored several churches and is
the author of many books and articles
focusing on the intersection of text,
church, and world. Estes is a regular
contributor to the science section of
Christianity Today and is the editor
of Faithlife's *Didaktikos: Journal of Theological Education.*
Connect with him at DouglasEstes.com, or follow him on
Twitter, @DouglasEstes.